"Getting organized and staying
in all aspects of life. This book

Chalene John
entrepreneu:

MW01001965

and 151 ivicuivu

"As a mother of seven, I can attest to a universal mom fact: the
struggle to organize the mayhem is real. Kristi Clover gets it, and
not only does she offer dozens of practical, simple ways to calm the
clutter and reclaim your joy but she reminds moms of this important truth: *everything is going to be okay.* Thanks, Kristi! I needed
this book!"

Heidi St. John, speaker, author of the Becoming MomStrong
series, and founder of MomStrong International

"Keeping everything in order on my never-ending to-do list of
motherhood can feel hopeless! In *M.O.M.—Master Organizer of
Mayhem*, Kristi Clover takes what seems overwhelmingly impossible and breaks it down into step-by-step systems to help busy
moms like me get organized! I love this highly practical and personal
resource! It is so needed for moms today."

Ruth Schwenk, founder of TheBetterMom.com,
author of *The Better Mom Devotional*,
and coauthor of *Pressing Pause* and *Settle My Soul*

"Everyone desires a home that radiates peace, joy, and love, yet too
often the 'stuff' of life takes over, cluttering every flat surface and
every crevice of our hearts. With wisdom, humor, and grace, Kristi
Clover provides practical advice for busy, overwhelmed moms. She
offers numerous ideas on how to discover organization techniques
that work for *your* life, based on *your* priorities. Spending time within
the pages of this book is like spending time with an organizational
coach, friend, and cheerleader all wrapped up into one. I highly
recommend this book!"

Tricia Goyer, *USA Today* bestselling author
of over seventy books, including *Calming Angry Kids*

"A messy home can make a mess out of a mom. We know it's true.
For years we've been ministering to parents who struggle with anger
at home each messy, chaotic day. Over and over again we've heard
that a messy house can be Mom's biggest 'trigger,' which is why
we're so excited about this new book! Kristi Clover doesn't just tell
us how to keep a tidy house but explains why bringing order to the

chaos is so important for the whole family. With personal stories that will keep you laughing (and turning the pages), Kristi teaches us simple solutions to bring order and joy into our home lives again."

Amber Lia and **Wendy Speake,** authors of *Triggers: Exchanging Parents' Angry Reactions for Gentle Biblical Responses* and *Parenting Scripts*

"Imagine if you were friends with someone who could help you reset the crazy in your life. Kristi Clover is that friend! In this joy-filled, practical, and easy-to-read book, you'll discover life-changing organizational secrets that can help make your life simply joyful."

Rhonda Stoppe, the "No Regrets Woman," author of *Moms Raising Sons to Be Men* and *The Marriage Mentor*

"I wish I had this book years ago. With five children and a busy schedule, I have always struggled with efficient home organization. With Kristi's relatable encouragement, I've already gleaned so many practical ideas that can be implemented immediately. *M.O.M.—Master Organizer of Mayhem* is a book that everyone can benefit from, no matter the ages of your children."

Jen Schmidt, author of *Just Open the Door,* host of the Becoming Conference, and blogger at *Balancing Beauty and Bedlam*

"Kristi is a breath of fresh air in this space! In this book she not only is your biggest cheerleader but also actually equips you with tactics and tools to succeed at managing the chaos. You'll finish it feeling encouraged and inspired—a must-read for modern mamas!"

Angela Braniff, mom of seven and creator of *This Gathered Nest*

"As a mother of five adult children, I know firsthand how important it is and how challenging it can be to organize and manage a home. In my experience, trying to get everything in its place can be downright frustrating at times. In *M.O.M.—Master Organizer of Mayhem*, Kristi gently takes moms by the hand and guides them step-by-step through the why and how of organizing. She takes complicated ideas and simplifies them. Her wit and humor, along with her transparency, will help mothers at any stage of parenting bring order to their life and home. I highly encourage mothers to read this book."

Connie Albers, author of *Parenting Beyond the Rules*

M.O.M.—
MASTER ORGANIZER *of* MAYHEM

Simple Solutions to Organize Chaos
and Bring More Joy into Your Home

KRISTI CLOVER

BakerBooks
a division of Baker Publishing Group
Grand Rapids, Michigan

© 2019 by Kristi Clover

Published by Baker Books
a division of Baker Publishing Group
PO Box 6287, Grand Rapids, MI 49516-6287
www.bakerbooks.com

Printed in the United States of America

Library of Congress Cataloging-in-Publication Data is on file at the Library of Congress, Washington, DC.

978-0-8010-9425-5

19 20 21 22 23 24 25   7 6 5 4 3 2 1

To my incredible husband, Steve.
There is no one I'd rather have by my side
on this journey of life. I love you
immeasurably.

To our amazing kids,
Grant, Blake, Wade, Ashlyn, and Caitlyn,
without whom I wouldn't carry the title
of mom (or M.O.M.). You and your dad
are the greatest blessings in my life.
I love you so much!

To my lifelong encourager, Mom.
It's because of your love and belief in me
that I dared to dream big.
What a blessing you are to me!

Contents

The Struggle Is Real!

Motherhood Changes Everything

There is no end to the great advice about organizing you can find online or in print. Inspiration is just a Google search away. Pinterest alone is full of beautiful quotes and motivational sayings. One of my favorites is the common saying, "A place for everything, everything in its place." But I've found that it doesn't matter if we have a place for everything if "everything" is thrown all around the house.

Motherhood adds a new dimension to the difficulty of staying organized. Getting organized is a challenge in and of itself, and keeping your house tidy just gets harder when there are several people living under one roof, whether the mess is due to our own bad habits, an untidy spouse, or our kids. We are a family of seven, and I like to say that our home has seven "moving parts," all of which increase the challenge of trying to keep a tidy house. Please note that I included my husband and myself in that number. Each person contributes in one way or another to both the order and disorder in our home—just to varying degrees.

Someone once said, "Cleaning with kids in the house is like trying to brush your teeth while eating Oreos." Maybe it's because I like

Oreos so much, but I love that quote. Something about it resonates with me and makes me want to shout, "Amen!" It's a perfect depiction of how I've felt about housekeeping since becoming a mom. It feels counterproductive to work hard to clean up when I know I'm going to have to start from scratch again the next day. Some days I feel like I'll never get on top of it all, despite my systems for keeping things organized and the job assignments I've given all my "helpers." When I don't stay on top of the daily clutter, it's easy to feel overwhelmed and inundated with the growing number of to-dos.

Motherhood Changes Everything

Feeling exhausted and overwhelmed is sometimes just par for the course when you have kids. Motherhood brings a lot of demands at all the various stages of parenting, yet there is no instruction manual on how to manage it all.

Many of us add to the weariness we're already feeling by creating unrealistic expectations for ourselves. We want a picture-perfect Joanna Gaines–style home and home-cooked meals that are worthy of Pioneer Woman Ree Drummond. We forget that these two TV sensations are not only gifted but also have teams of helpers on set with them. However, no matter who we compare ourselves to, when we allow ourselves to make other people our gold standard for how things should be done, we set ourselves up for disappointment.

When I first became a mom, I had Martha Stewart breathing down my neck. This homemaking, party-planning maven graced the pages of most popular magazines and TV shows with her perfectly set tables and five-course meals all created from scratch with food from her two-acre garden. Okay, so I have no idea how large her garden really was at that time. However, it didn't change the fact that I felt this need to live up to some "picture" of what homemaking was supposed to look like. Try as I might, I just couldn't—and I was exhausted trying.

Today we have Pinterest, Instagram, Facebook, blogs, magazines, television shows, books, and more telling us how we are supposed to manage our homes. Much of the advice on home management and organization isn't written with moms in mind. It tends to be too broad-reaching. There's also an underlying misconception that if we just declutter here and there, then we will have order in our house. The problem is, we all literally have "moving parts" in our homes. Little hands and little feet that find ways to undo all our hard work. Sometimes, even the big hands of older kids or our spouses move things around. As most families have come to find out, we can declutter our house from top to bottom and still feel completely unorganized a few days later. There is just a different dynamic at play when there is more than one person living in a home.

Hitting the Reset Button

My heart with this book is to help you adjust your expectations for yourself, your family, and your home. As a mom of five, I understand how it feels to have your household feel out of control at times. I also know it's tempting to continue to put off getting organized and save it for another day. Unfortunately, the longer we delay getting started, the more chaotic things become and the greater our stress.

> I crave the simplicity that organization brings, as I'm sure you do. But even more than the simplicity, I long for the joy and peace that wait on the other side of crazy.

I want my home to breathe life into all who enter and live here. I want to create an atmosphere that radiates love and a place where my family wants to be. Knowing these goals helps

11

motivate me to do the work necessary to bring about that simplicity, joy, and peace.

Believe it or not, our mindset is one of the key ingredients to getting our house in order. I had to hit rock bottom before I was ready to figure out how to better manage my home. I'll talk more about that defining moment in the next chapter, but for now let's just say that I hope you don't have to hit an all-time low too before you make some changes. If you're reading this and thinking, *I'm there! I can't take this anymore!* then you're in the right place.

Regardless of what made you pick up this book—utter frustration with the daily mayhem or an insatiable desire to learn all you can about organization—you are in for a treat. I tend to approach things differently than most people do. I love dissecting things and simplifying them. I'm also keenly aware that not every person or family is the same. We all have different family dynamics and priorities. All of that plays into how we organize our lives and our homes—and how we make these new organizational habits stick.

Some people are just naturally organized or have been brought up with amazing habits. However, that is not me. I had some bad habits to break. It's taken me a lot of trial and error—*and effort*—to dig myself out of the disorder I created.

I'm a bit of an oxymoron. I'm the messiest neat-freak you'll ever meet and a lazy perfectionist. Plus, I'm highly analytical and creative. It's as though my right and left brain are constantly at war. Yet I've learned it's okay to be a little of both. Consequently, when it comes to my approach to getting things done, I am both creative and practical. That means I am not just going to throw theories at you for how to get organized without giving you several specific ways to apply what I'm talking about.

Because there really isn't a one-size-fits-all approach to home organization, I'm also going to give you lots of useful methods to try in your home. That way you can see what options work best for you and your family.

Building Order—and Efficiency—into Your Home

When building a house, a critical first step is laying a solid foundation. Organizing a home is no different. In phase I, "The Foundation," we'll be discussing my "top ten" rules for building order in your home. These rules comprise the foundation for getting organized. In phase II, "The Framework," we'll get into the nitty-gritty techniques and systems that act as the framework for getting things done efficiently. In phase III, "The Finishing Touches," we'll be talking about how to make your home both *functional* and *fabulous* with intentional decorating.

I first presented my "top ten" list thirteen years ago during a home organization workshop that I gave to a large moms' group in my area. What's interesting is that all these years later, only the order of the list has changed. I laugh now when I think about those early M.O.M. workshops. My boys were four and three at the time, and I didn't have a clue what was in store for me in a few short years—three more kids who would become three more "moving parts" in our household and substantially increase our potential for messes. Since then, I've had plenty of time to apply these ten rules and try out different methods and systems.

One thing to keep in mind is that all of these sections—or building phases—were designed to fit together. None stand alone. We can declutter all we want, but if our priorities are out of whack then we will end up right back where we started—frustrated and overwhelmed. We can even implement some of the systems for getting organized, but if we aren't tweaking them for our own personality and family, we may want to just give up.

The foundation, framework, and finishing touches work together in your home regardless of how many people you have in the mix. Whether you live alone or have tons of kids, the tips and techniques in this book can help you bring some order to your chaos—as long as you apply them!

This book is designed to be an ongoing resource for you to use in your journey of organizing your home. Think of it as a set of blueprints that you'll refer to as you build order and efficiency into your home. One of the key elements you'll find at the end of chapters 2 through 17 is a section called **Unlocking Joy**. These segments are meant to encourage you to make decisions and start taking action on what you are learning. You don't have to do everything all at once. Just have fun with it: the goal is to transform your home and "unlock" more joy.

I've also included numerous **Toolbox Tips**, which are additional ideas to tuck away in your "organizational toolbox."

YOU'VE GOT THIS!

It's never too late to hit the reset button. You can climb out of the mayhem and conquer the clutter. It may seem like a daunting task, but it's so worth the effort. Beyond that, it's very doable. Staying organized is a never-ending task, just like doing the laundry and dishes, but you can find more efficient ways of doing tasks within your home. That's what we're going to focus on: simple solutions to our homemaking challenges that bring order to our home and open the door to joy—and fun! We'll talk about that too. Fun always makes things easier.

We're in this together. My season of having our kids living in our home is far from over. I'm in the trenches with you. I get it. I know the struggle is real. So let's get started! I can't wait for you to jump in and join me on this quest to become M.O.M.s: Master Organizers of Mayhem!

1

Embracing Your Inner Organizer

Discovering Your Hidden Potential

My tears were falling so fast I had to pull over to the side of the road. Heaven forbid my sobbing cause an accident, especially with my babies in the car. I'd only made it about two blocks from my house before the dam broke loose.

I had never felt this overwhelmed in my life. I wasn't prepared for it. I had called my dear friend Renee as I was backing my car out of the driveway of our new house, but her name was all I could manage to say before the onslaught of heavy sobs began. I had no words. Only tears.

"Oh, Kristi, how can I help? I don't know what to do! I don't know what to do!" Renee had never heard me this upset before. She was at a loss for how to calm me down enough to find out why I was so upset.

So much was happening on every front of my life. We had recently moved to a new city, away from my family, our best friends, and the home that we thought we'd grow old in. My husband's travel schedule had been doubled with our move, so Steve was not home much. Most of the time, I was home alone with our two babies, trying to get us settled. Grant was twenty-one months old and Blake was four months old. In the span of those few months since Blake had been born, I had two unexpected surgeries, Steve had an emergency surgery, our car was hit in a parking garage, Grant got the stomach flu, the construction of our new house was behind schedule, we were having problems at the apartment we were renting, we had stress in our marriage, our seventy-pound dog seemed to forget how to go to the bathroom outside—and more. It was the perfect storm for my complete breakdown. I felt unsettled, exhausted, and out of control.

When we were told we could finally move into our new home, I thought that things would get better. However, they only got more complicated. On move-in day, we discovered that our newly constructed house was not fully inhabitable. Most of our big "final walk-through" items had not been taken care of. It was winter and the house had no heat, no interior doors, and no hot water, for starters. The house still needed weeks, which turned into months, of work. As the builders tried to fix one problem they either created or discovered a whole new problem. Plus, most of the other stresses and issues were still present. Since there was no way to stop escrow from closing or the moving vans from arriving, we just tried to make the best of it.

That set the stage for why I was crying, but it leaves out the best part of the story. Right before I backed out of the garage, called Renee, and sat curbside bawling . . . well, I made another phone call. I called the project manager for our house. Poor man.

"Hello, Kristi. How are you doing?" he answered cheerfully.

"Not good! I have tried to be a good Christian and be patient and kind as I've waited for you to address the needs of our home. Well, that's not working. So if you don't get a team of guys over here in the next hour, I'm going to lose it.

"Do you hear that? That is the sound of my baby screaming! He's crying because he's hungry—and I'm so stressed out that my milk won't let down." (Yes, I really said that!)

"I'm leaving the house," I continued. "I expect to see your men here when I return."

Click.

When I returned home, there was a team of workers running around my house getting things done. When the project manager walked over to me, I wanted to crawl under a rock. I had spoken to him in such an unkind way . . . and, well, there was that comment about my milk.

"Uhh . . . so . . . we're here. Sorry we made you feel like you weren't important to our team," he said. "And . . . well . . . uhh . . . is your milk okay?"

We both started laughing.

I was so embarrassed, but by that night, when I tried to explain my day to Steve, we couldn't stop laughing about that conversation. My husband has my favorite laugh in the whole world: a knee-slapping, from-the-gut kind of laugh. And my story got him going, which in turn got me going.

While that was one of my darkest days, it was also the day I realized something had to change. That was my moment. The moment I admitted I wasn't a "super mom" and couldn't get everything done. The moment I acknowledged that while I couldn't control or change all the circumstances in my life, I could change some things. I could bring some order to our home—and I could change my attitude. Yep, *attitude.* It has everything to do with finding the motivation to get organized. It also has everything to do with experiencing more joy.

I learned how to better organize our lives and our home out of sheer necessity. I had to hit rock bottom before I found the determination to figure out some ways to bring about order in my chaos. So my research started . . . and my passion for organization was ignited.

Redefining *Organization*

When I first started speaking on home organization, I felt a bit like a hypocrite because my house wasn't perfectly organized all the time. I only saw what needed to be done and felt like we constantly had toys thrown around everywhere. Yet this was always the topic people wanted me to talk about. Friends consistently told me how organized I was and asked me for advice on home management. And the truth was, I loved organizing. It was a passion that had grown through that hard season. As I found relief from one area of frustration in my house, I then set to work on conquering another area. I researched how different people did things and tweaked them to work in my home.

As I prepared to speak at that first moms' group, I sat down with all of the notes I had taken through the years and asked myself, *What key principles have I implemented that helped create this* perception *that I'm so organized?*

Do you like how I put that? I'm absolutely serious. I didn't feel like I had come to a point of mastery in my homemaking. Somehow, others saw me differently than I saw myself. After that first workshop, I was blown away by the number of moms who thanked me for my advice . . . many in tears. Here I thought I was exposing myself as a fraud by being honest about how I'd had to learn to let things go. Yes, I shared lots of practical tips on meal planning, housecleaning, and home management, but I tried hard to be very real at the same time.

Here's the truth I learned that day: *most moms feel like failures in their homes.* Maybe not in every area but usually in at least one aspect of home life. We all struggle, because mess happens. And it keeps happening. Over and over again. To top it off, we are tired. Sometimes we just don't have the energy or the willpower to tidy up at the end of a long day.

I also began to understand that we tend to equate being organized with perfection. Yet that's not what organization is at all. Please get rid of this notion! Being organized *does not* mean we have to have a perfect home, sterile and clean, at all times. Clean is good, but dust bunnies, crumbs, and spilled milk happen— sometimes even spilled organic milk. (Okay, so it does hurt a bit more when it's the expensive, organic brand that is splashed across the floor, but you get my point!)

Here's how I view organization:

> Organization is about increasing the efficiency in our home so that we can maximize our time with our family and for other priorities.

Notice that nothing in this definition implies perfection. Maybe I should have called this chapter "Embracing Your Inner Elsa," because we need to learn to "let go" of this idea of "perfect"—and give ourselves some grace. Every mother knows that staying on top of the daily mess is hard work. Exhausting work! Whether you have one child or twenty! Just when you think you have the house organized, cleaned, and looking good, the kids wake up. And there are some seasons when it's just harder to stay on top of the mess. In those times, we need to realize that something has to give, and we may need to lower our expectations for what our home looks like and how smoothly our days should go. These are also the exact seasons when some of the systems we'll be talking about in phase II can help us to stay as organized as we can.

The more we learn how to streamline and simplify things in our home, the less stress we will feel. Less stress equals a happier mom. A happier mom equals a happier home. (Note: it may not mean fewer toddler tantrums, just fewer mommy tantrums!)

———— YOU'VE GOT THIS! ————

Don't let your past feelings of failure or your current situation of frustration hold you back from experiencing the freedom and joy that can come from getting your home to run more smoothly. You can learn to be organized, whether you have natural tendencies for it or not. I know because that is what happened to me. In fact, my life *now* looks nothing like what I experienced in my childhood. (More about that in the next chapter!)

I believe that we all have the potential to be amazing organizers. We all have this inner organizer who just needs to be awakened. She doesn't always want to be bothered, though, which is why once she's been stirred from her sleep we need to embrace her. I used the word *embrace* deliberately. To embrace something is to clasp it, hold on to it, and wrap our arms around it. There is an intentional element to organizing. Order doesn't just happen. We need to strip away old habits and replace them with routines and systems that we can tweak to work in our own homes.

Together we are going to find our inner organizer and get her to stick around without worrying that she's going to run for the hills at the first sign of imperfection. So let's jump in and start learning ten simple rules that can revolutionize how we organize our home.

Phase I

THE
FOUNDATION

Ten Simple Rules That Will
Change Your Home Life

Rule #1: Use the "Glean and Tweak" Technique

Don't Start from Scratch

I should probably admit right up front that I have a snarky side. Most of the time I try to contain it. Usually I just make myself giggle as great comebacks come to mind. I'll only say them out loud if I know I'm not going to offend anyone . . . and if it will get a good laugh.

My family is not your standard California family. Number one, we have five kids. Number two, we homeschool. Mentioning either of these two fun facts about my family often brings out strange reactions from people. One of the funniest moments was when I was pregnant with our fifth child. Apparently, I missed the memo that you are not supposed to have any more children if you already have at least one boy and one girl.

When I was pregnant with Ashlyn, our first girl, people would look at my three boys and say, "Oh, you must be trying for a girl," or "Did you finally get your girl?" These comments didn't bother me too much. My pregnancy seemed to be "acceptable" to those around me. Four was still a lot, but apparently if you are trying for a different gender, it is okay to keep having babies. However, that was not the case when I was pregnant with number five. As I ran errands with all my kids, people would see my very large belly, count my kids, notice that I already had boys *and* one girl, and exclaim, "Why are you pregnant? You already have your girl!" It got a little tiring. I started thinking of great comebacks to their comments, though I rarely shared them.

However, one day a complete stranger laughed at me and said, "That's a lot of kids! You do know what causes that, right?" Yes, I know he was being funny, but on that particular day, in my hormonal, pregnant state, I opened my mouth and dropped a little sample of my snarkiness. (That's not a word, but I guess it is now, since it's in this book! Look at me transforming the written language.)

I looked at my beautiful children and said, "Well, *you* know what they say—'practice makes perfect.'" The man was speechless. I think I made the woman behind him blush. I just smiled and walked away. Of course, then I was left with children asking me what that meant.

Nowadays, I usually don't take all my kids to the store with me. So instead of having to contend with people counting my kids, I contend with them counting the gallons of milk in my cart. Yep! I cause quite a stir when I go grocery shopping. My cart is usually overflowing. I often hear things like, "Are you feeding a football team?" or, "Man, you must be having a party!" Yes, I am! A 24/7 party is always happening at the Clover house. And although we aren't feeding a football team, we are feeding a lot of mouths. I know most people mean nothing by their comments and are just being playful. Yet sometimes I want to be playful too.

So, one time, just one time, I decided to say something I'd been storing up. "How in the world do you manage a home with *that* many children?" a sweet woman once asked, gasping, after I told her the size of our family.

"Easy," I replied with a slight smile. "Martha Stewart is my mom."

The look on her face. . . . I burst out laughing. When I fessed up to the fact that I was kidding, her laughter joined mine. I had picked the perfect person for my playful antics.

Overcoming Childhood Habits

Now that we've established I was not brought up in a homemaking dynasty, I should tell you that my life now looks *nothing* like it did when I was young. I was an only child raised by a single, working mom, and I was anything but organized.

When I was growing up, my mom worked long hours to provide for the two of us. She was (and still is) one of my heroes. Late work nights meant that I usually walked to a friend's house after school to hang out until my mom got off work. Many nights I fixed myself macaroni and cheese or canned beef ravioli for dinner.

For the record, my mom was a master at making the most of our time together. I have many incredible memories of all the fun we had when I was growing up. She could make everyday moments special, and I learned so much from her about how to do the same. My mom also taught me how to clean the house. I could make a bathroom sink shine. However, as much as she tried to get me to pick up after myself, *decluttering* was not in my vocabulary. My room was a natural disaster. I had so many bad habits. I never made my bed, despite my mom's wise advice that "The bed is the largest thing in the room, and when it's made the whole room looks cleaner." Somehow my clothes never seemed to make it into the hamper. I had one clear spot on the floor that I used to leap from the doorway to my bed. When there was time to clean up, it was the last thing I wanted to do, so I continued to ignore the mess. I had the rest of the house to hang out in, so my room could wait.

It wasn't until I was in college that I learned I had a knack for organizing. I had always loved packing our car for trips and making everything magically fit but had never thought much of it. However, when I was forced to live in a small room with another person, my inner organizer suddenly emerged. When my high school friends came to visit me, they were shocked by how clean my room was. Even so, I still didn't know the first thing about creating habits to help me stay on top of the mess.

The Game Changer

One thing to know about me—well, yet another thing to know about me—is the fact that I love researching things. I'm crazy that way. I love to learn all I can about new things I jump into. When Steve and I were first married, I read tons of books on marriage. When we started having babies, I learned all I could about pregnancy, newborn care, and parenting. Oh, and I was that crazy woman who actually did prepare for a roadside birth when I was pregnant with our first. I not only kept my hospital bag in the back of the car but a "just in case I give birth in my car" bag as well.

When I realized I needed to get more organized in order to survive, I started researching. I scoured the internet, bought a few books, and borrowed more books from the library. I started asking questions too. I tried to figure out who in my life seemed to manage their home well.

I tried several of the suggested tips and techniques, but things kept going back to crazy. How was it that these tried-and-true methods weren't working for me? I was getting frustrated.

Then my game-changing moment came. Instead of giving up, I started tweaking the ideas and information I'd gathered from books and from conversations with friends and family. I started

TOOLBOX TIP

When you're reading this book (or any other book on home organization), star, underline, and highlight things that stand out to you. When you find techniques you want to implement or have your own ideas come to you as you read, write them down in the back of the book. This will save you time when you are ready to try out some of the tips you learned. No more flipping through the book to find your inspired thoughts. They're all in one spot. For this book, I've included a special Take Note! section for you on page 227.

It's also helpful to keep all your favorite books on home management in one spot on a bookshelf.

synthesizing what I'd learned and began coming up with ways to make all the advice work efficiently for *my* family.

The "Glean and Tweak" Technique

Home organization isn't a one-size-fits-all thing. I believe this misconception is one of the primary reasons most organizational habits don't work for some of us. Fancy planners, decluttering, and set routines only work if they sync with your individual bent and your unique family circumstances. Some systems just don't offer long-term results if you can't personalize or "tweak" them to fit with your natural tendencies.

We are all unique in how we approach things, so it's critical to learn the skill of gleaning from what works well for some families and then tweaking it to make it fit your own family's dynamics. **The most important thing to know is that you may have to try a few different techniques before you find the right match.** You may even have to tweak things a few more times as your family changes and grows. However, that's the beauty of learning to "glean and tweak." You stop feeling like a failure and instead look at what's not working as an indicator that it's time to change things up again.

We've probably all been told, "Don't reinvent the wheel," or "Don't start from scratch." Let's face it: we are moms. Time is not always on our side. Since we don't have an abundance of time to get things done, it never hurts to ask other people for tips on how they do things or what works for them. I refer to the people who I go to for advice as my "homemaking mentors."

Of course, nowadays ideas and inspiration are everywhere online. Pinterest is jam-packed with great, albeit sometimes over-the-top, ideas. This book is also the perfect place to start doing some gleaning. I've come up with a lot of systems on my own, but I've also learned how other people do things and have figured out ways to adapt their organizational approaches to work better in my home.

Think of gleaning as your inspiration springboard. **The purpose of gleaning is to gather information and ideas from friends, family, books, Pinterest, or wherever you can about how to better organize your home life.** The goal is to learn methods that work for other people. Don't be surprised if you get very different advice or even conflicting advice.

> "Only do laundry once a week."
> "Do one load of laundry each day."
> "Don't start a new load of laundry until the last load is completely done: washed, dried, folded, and put away."
> "Assign each person in the house their own day to get laundry done." (This one's mine, by the way!)

Each of these tips is great for helping some families get the laundry done—but not every family. For example, there is no possible way my family could get all of our laundry done in one day. And it would drive me crazy to have to do one load of laundry every single day. I need a break from laundry. And that's why I am sold on the technique of gleaning and tweaking. Gleaning allows you to gather up a host of ideas to consider and then decide which ones to try out. Once you have a few ideas of which systems or techniques you'd like to try, then it's time to tweak.

To better understand what I mean by tweaking, think about how you approach cooking or baking. If a recipe calls for ingredients you know your family doesn't enjoy, you wouldn't hesitate to change it. You'd add things, leave things out, or change it up completely to create your own variation of the recipe. What you may end up with is a culinary masterpiece that your whole family loves. **This is what tweaking is all about: figuring out what works best for you and your family.**

There is no cookie-cutter answer when it comes to how to organize your home. My brain may be wired differently from yours. What has worked for me may not work for you. In addition, what works for your family when your kids are babies may be very different from what will work when they are teens. And what works in a small house will be different from what works in a large house. Homes with little storage space require creativity and a bit more minimalistic thinking than homes with plenty of storage. It's also true that an overabundance of storage space can thwart our ability to truly be organized. People who have extra drawers, cupboards, closets, or even extra space in their garage tend to fill up that space with things they don't need or have forgotten about. I call this "organized clutter." Organized clutter is the "out of sight and out of mind" assortment of odds and ends that we have tucked away somewhere. But here's the thing: organized clutter is still clutter.

The most important thing about learning how to best organize *your* home is not to give up. If something isn't working, then tweak what you're doing or try something else. You don't have to stay stuck. You can get more organized. There may just be a little trial and error involved in the process.

Beware: Don't Compare!

As you are perusing Pinterest, checking out blog posts, or even visiting a friend who has a clutter-free home, fight the urge to compare other people's successes with your frustrations. You may just be in a different season of life. Also, please trust me when I say that the internet lies. Bloggers are known for clearing a messy spot to get a good shot with great lighting, then just piling things right back where they were. (Or maybe that's just me. Ha! With seven people in our house, there are days when our home looks like it has been hit by a hurricane.)

Remember, perfection is not the goal. The goal is to create more efficiency and order in your home. Give yourself some grace. Allow the success of others to inspire rather than deflate you. You might consider going on a social media fast to get all the "perfection" out of sight for a little bit.

Organizing Your Gleaning and Tweaking

As you gather information, I encourage you to create a file for all your home organization notes—whether digitally or in a file folder. When I first started gleaning information, I clipped magazine articles and pictures and stuck them all in a file folder. Now,

TOOLBOX TIP

Another great place to glean and store ideas is Pinterest. I have a board for all the fun, creative "home organization" blog posts I find—and another board for recipes that look tasty. Create as many boards as you'd like to categorize all the good storage tips, cleaning tips, or organizational solutions you find online. You can use Pinterest as a search engine as well. Just type in whatever you are looking for into the search bar and you'll see a ton of articles pop up.

this method still works, but technology has opened up other ways of doing things. I've started using an app called OneNote as my digital notebook. I have the app on my computer and my phone. It makes it easy to jot down ideas, drop in photos, and add links to great articles I find. I can even scan magazine articles to a file on the app. I created one tab in OneNote for all my home organization ideas and another tab for interior decorating ideas. Evernote is another popular digital notebook app that is similar. Using a digital notebook is convenient once you get the hang of it.

Practice Makes Progress

As you glean and tweak ideas for how you can bring more efficiency into your home, don't focus on how to do things perfectly. Instead, focus on forward momentum and the progress you are making.

} Forget about all the things on your to-do list
} that aren't done yet. Focus on the things you
} are accomplishing.

If you have tried one thing and it didn't work well, chalk it up to a bad week. Maybe you need to try a different system or technique to see if it fits better for you and your family in the phase of life you are in. The key is to just keep practicing what you are learning.

────────────── **YOU'VE GOT THIS!** ──────────────

Don't give up or get stuck thinking you'll never be good at organizing. Regardless of your background or the bad habits you may have, you can learn new techniques that will work for your home. Just remember that you and your family are unique. I like to remind myself that one of my ultimate goals in getting organized is to create an environment of peace and joy in my home. When my house is organized, I am more likely to relax and enjoy my family—and to open my home to others. Home organization doesn't have to be daunting, and it doesn't have to be boring. You just have to get started—and keep making progress.

So start gleaning from this and other books, the internet, and friends, then look for ways to tweak aspects of those systems to work best for your home.

Unlocking Joy

Welcome to the first Unlocking Joy section. As you begin to "master the mayhem" by implementing what you are learning, you'll be unlocking joy in your home. To help you start taking action, I've created some great printables that go hand in hand with the Unlocking Joy sections. Why start from scratch when I've already done all the work for you? Plus, the printables are really pretty. Just head over to **KristiClover.com/MOMPrintables** to access them.

Now it's time to roll up your sleeves and get started!

1. **Decide if you will keep your organizational ideas digitally or in a physical file (or both).**

   ☐ Digital File   ☐ File Folder

2. **Create a list of what you need to learn and what you want to learn.** Maybe your problem area, like mine, is paper piles, or maybe it's cleaning techniques or kitchen organization. You might even have baking or gardening on your wish-I-knew-how-to-do list. Just write it down below. This will help you narrow your focus to what you need to be researching.

I need to learn:

_____

_____

_____

I want to learn:

_____

_____

_____

3. Who in your life would make a great homemaking mentor?

_____

_____

_____

Rule #2: Don't Forget Your Top Priorities

Choosing Which Balls to Drop

Steve's greatest "I told you so" moment came six days after the birth of our fourth child. You should know that when we first purchased the house we're currently living in, I had envisioned hosting a wedding in our backyard someday. So when a friend wanted to use our backyard for her wedding, it was a dream come true. As she and her fiancé stood before Steve and me, all starry-eyed with their enthusiasm bubbling over, they told us that they wanted to get married on July 23. That was only a few months away—as was my due date—July 31. (Yep. You've already guessed how this played out, haven't you?)

Since she was a teacher, they didn't have a lot of flexibility on their dates. They needed to get married in the summer before the new school year started. I rubbed my pregnant belly as I stood there thinking it over. I looked up at Steve, who knew I really wanted to host this wedding. He was looking back at me like I was crazy. I then looked at the couple, feeling almost as much excitement about finally having a wedding in my backyard as they had for their wedding day.

When I told them that my due date was only a week after their wedding, my friend suggested that they find another location. However, I was adamant that the date would work. I reassured them that I'd never gone into labor early and promised to even ask my doctor about it.

Later that night, Steve tried with every analytical bone in his body to help me look at things pragmatically. He even wisely pointed out that other wedding venues would not accept bookings if they were already booked—and we were booked. Our calendar said we had something else going on during that time: a new baby coming. Please note my husband's effort to use wedding lingo with me. I thought it was so sweet. However, in my little-organized brain, I had it all worked out. We could host the wedding on the twenty-third, then I could be induced on the twenty-fifth. (Long story on why I was being induced.)

The wedding plans went along smoothly. My husband worked so hard to make our backyard look extra beautiful. I worked on creating some space inside our house for the wedding party to use to get ready. And although everyone in my life kept saying I was insane for hosting a wedding so close to my due date, I insisted it would all be fine.

It was one week before the wedding—and my birthday. Throughout the day, I noticed that my Braxton-Hicks contractions were getting more consistent and more intense. But it was my birthday, so I tried to ignore them. That evening Steve took our family to Benihana's. He had even picked up my favorite Oreo ice cream cake and had it waiting at home for us. (I told you I liked Oreos!) My mom had just gotten into town to celebrate my birthday and to help with the wedding and new baby. So the evening was extra special.

About halfway through dinner a mother and daughter who were seated at the hibachi table with us looked at me with big eyes and asked, "Are you timing your contractions? They seem to be really close together." I giggled, because I had started timing them but didn't realize they were so obvious. Apparently I would stop mid-sentence to breathe and then would just keep talking once it went by. I had a wedding to get through, and close contractions weren't on the schedule.

But by the time we got home, I knew I was in labor. Okay, I'd known at dinner, but I was in denial. My contractions were strong and not letting up—and were two minutes apart. I was grateful I'd already packed my hospital bag but regretted that I hadn't installed the car seat yet. So as Steve scrambled to pack his own hospital bag, I installed the baby's car seat while having strong contractions. Not my best moment, but I did find humor in the fact that I could barely move the seat into place with my big belly in the way. It must have been quite a sight.

Yes, the following afternoon we were holding Ashlyn in our arms. My first birthday buddy was born—just six days before the wedding. Even though the wedding was beautiful and special, my insistence on hosting caused a lot of unnecessary stress for our family.

While my husband never did actually say, "I told you so," he didn't need to. I already knew it. Not only had I overcommitted but I also had failed to keep my priorities straight. I put serving others and my "dream come true" before protecting my family's needs and schedule.

Juggling Wisely

Nothing brings more chaos to a home than an overly busy schedule and an overladen to-do list. Most of us moms attempt to keep as many proverbial balls in the air as we can, but in truth we only have the capacity to keep a few up at one time. That was the case with me hosting a wedding only days before I was due to have a baby. Yes, I had a plan for how to pull off both masterfully. That's what kept me going. However, once Ashlyn came early, it was game over. All the remaining prep on my end fell on everyone else in my family—mostly Steve. While we felt honored to share in such a special day with our friends, I shouldn't have said yes knowing the wedding was so close to my due date.

As much as trying to multitask is praised, glorified, and sought after, it is not the best thing for families. Doing too much sets us up for unnecessary frustration and failure. Family life requires a certain amount of juggling. The more people in your home, the more things can creep into your schedule. The key is to juggle wisely.

I know I can only do so much. We all have a limit to what we can accomplish. No one can "do it all," yet that's what we seem to think everyone else is doing, so we try to do it too. But let me share a secret with you: you can get only the most important things done and still have an incredible sense of fulfillment. I mean this both in your life and in your home. But for this to happen you have to look at your schedule and evaluate it in light of your priorities and goals. Are the activities you are saying yes to the activities that are most important to you and your family? What might you need to cut in order to reach your goals?

Here's the thing:

> Prioritizing is the key to masterful multitasking—or should I say juggling? When we are intentional about which "balls" to set aside for a time and which to focus on, we are unburdened and free to feel more successful in our home life.

If we don't first declutter our schedules, we'll never find the time to declutter our homes. Both kinds of decluttering are equally important. In both cases, the less we have to organize—and juggle—the easier it is to stay on top of things.

The "Four Leaves" of First Importance

Through the years I've talked online and at speaking engagements about our family's top priorities. We identified them in the process of writing our family's mission statement, but they have become a yardstick for how we measure where things in our lives fall within our family's priorities. Knowing our top priorities helps us to figure out what we can say yes to and what we need to say no to. It also helps us identify what has to be done now and what can wait or be skipped altogether.

Since we are the Clover family, we tend to do things in fours, like a four-leaf clover. Our four "leaves," in the order of importance, are:

**FAITH
FAMILY
FRIENDS
FELLOW MAN**

As a Christian family, our faith is our first priority. If we're so busy that we're not growing our faith by spending time reading the Bible and praying, then we need to slow down or reprioritize our days. Similarly, if we are serving too much outside our home and neglecting time with family, then something has to change. If we have friends who are in need of some TLC, then we need to cut back on outside ministries or activities.

Regardless of whether or not you are a person of faith, you need to figure out what your priorities are in order of importance.

Feel free to use our family's 4Fs or create your own measuring stick for your family's priorities. I've found that life is much smoother when we live out our priorities instead of trying to do every little thing that comes our way.

Let me show you how our 4Fs help our family prioritize. Our family is pretty athletic, and Steve and I love having our kids participate in sports. But we've found that when we have multiple kids in sports at the same time with multiple practice times and games, we have no downtime for our family. So when basketball season comes and our kids are not able to play on the same team, we typically pull back on our other outside-the-home activities. There have also been times when we've taken a break from sports altogether in order to put family first. We've never regretted those moments.

For us, sports fall under the last "F" (fellow man) since we are spending time with other people more than with family and friends. However, if Steve is coaching the team, if it's a family sporting activity, or if the kids are on a team with lots of friends, then the activity moves up in order of importance.

Each individual family has to decide what their priorities are and how to use them to evaluate what to say yes to and what to say no to. There are always going to be lots of wonderful things to add to our schedules, but we need to carefully think through what the best things are so we don't overcommit ourselves or our family.

How Important Is Home Management?

Perhaps you're wondering, *Where does home management fit in with my priorities?* Great question. Now, what I'm about to say might just blow your mind. Wait for it . . .

> There will be seasons when managing your home
> needs to take a backseat in order to ensure you

are living out your priorities. However, there are
also times when your lack of home management can
keep you from using your home to welcome and
encourage others.

Complicated, isn't it? You might be feeling a sense of relief to
hear me say that spending time with your family and friends is
more important than obsessing over the state of your home. Too
many people get caught up in this idea that their house needs to
be perfect in order to open their doors to others.

While you may have heard people say that they "bless" with
their "mess"—and there is a bit of truth there—I want to tweak it
a bit and say that we *can* bless even if there is mess. **The people
in our lives need to know they are more important to us than
a perfectly organized home.** Our kids love hanging out with
us more than they love that the dishes are clean and put away.
The girlfriend who needs a shoulder to cry on probably won't
notice the pile of laundry beside her on the couch. It's okay for
your house to look lived in.

But here's where the second part of my statement comes in:
there are times when the mess becomes too much of a disrup-
tion. While I think it's totally fine for my homemaking to take
a backseat from time to time when life is busy or people need
me, if I let it go for too long it just adds to the stress level in my
home. We start tripping over piles, things get lost or broken, and
there is no real sense of peace to be found. We can handle it for
a while, but over time it's too much. When I start noticing that
the house is becoming a source of tension, that is my cue to start
focusing more attention on managing my home and stop putting
things off. Plus, there is a level of cleanliness that probably should
not go overlooked for too long.

Everyone is wired differently. Some care too much and others
may not care enough. But you are the judge of your own situation.

It doesn't matter to me whether your home is in pristine condition or in a state of chaos. I'm not judging you, and no one else should either. Motherhood is hard. Making time to organize your home is a balancing act. But that's why I'm writing this book. I want to help you figure out what your goals are and help you to achieve them.

Remember how I redefined *organization*? It is increasing the efficiency in our home so that we can maximize our time with our family and for other priorities. We can be overconsumed with cleaning and organizing and miss opportunities to spend time with our family and friends—or we may not be mindful enough of our home management and send others the message, "Please don't come to my house." Either way, we can miss out on moments to connect with those important to us.

Understanding Our "Why"

Probably the most powerful element to finding success in any new endeavor is understanding our "why." Whatever we are trying to accomplish, be it home organization or learning a new language, we will never find the motivation we need to make changes and follow through until we see the value in it. That's why asking ourselves why we want to be organized is so important.

When we know why we want to become more organized, it helps us to change our mindset. Suddenly, our goals become a catalyst for actually accomplishing what we want to get done. Remember how my need for sanity during my "dark days" became my goal during that time? Well, sanity is still one of the main reasons I like to have order in my home. But don't be surprised if you need to ask yourself again and again what your goals are for your home, because our whys can change through the years.

My goal in organizing my home is to create a welcoming atmosphere of love, joy, and peace. I want my home to be a place where my husband and kids choose to be. Beyond that, I want people who visit my house to feel at home. I try to create an inviting environment. I don't want piles to deter me from my ability to minister to others. Plus, the more organized I am, the less time I waste scrambling around before guests arrive. There have been some seasons, such as when I had newborns or toddlers, when it felt impossible to stay on top of everything. But I've found that by implementing systems in our home that keep us more organized, I'm better prepared for all the different seasons ahead.

Special Note: if you are in the newborn stage of motherhood (or have other crazy circumstances going on in life), please just focus on taking care of yourself and your family. The house can wait. Maybe skip to the chapter on asking for help. Just take a deep breath, then slowly let it out—and maybe go take a good nap.

Determining Your Household Priorities

One night years ago, I was racing around trying to pull the house together so that it would feel warm and welcoming for Steve when he got home from a long business trip. I never want him to walk in the door and wish he was back in a hotel again. Well, it'd been a crazy week with the kids, appointments, and just life. I was so tired and had let the house go. Dishes had piled up, toys hadn't been put away, and the previous night's empty pizza boxes were still on the counter. I looked around and realized there was no way for me to get it all done before he got home. As he walked in the door, instead of greeting him with a happy hug, I broke down in tears in his arms. I felt like a failure . . . as though I'd let him down in some way.

I should probably back up a moment and explain that Steve's love language is acts of service.* This basically means that he

---

*"Love languages" is a popular term used to describe how we communicate and interpret love and is based on the book *The Five Love Languages* by Gary Chapman. The five love languages are acts of service, physical touch, words of affirmation, quality time, and receiving gifts.

appreciates it when people do special things for him. (Me? Well, I'm a physical touch and words of affirmation girl. Just give me a big hug and tell me you love me and think I'm both beautiful and amazing, and my love tank gets filled.) The problem was, I was putting all this dysfunctional pressure on myself by thinking that Steve would only feel loved if I had the house perfect all the time . . . and dinner ready . . . and the toys picked up . . . and . . . and . . . and. . . . He'd never asked for this. I had this ill-conceived notion that I had to "perform" and be great at everything in order to be a good wife and mom.

That night I asked him a question I'd never thought to ask before. (Silly me!) I asked him what he appreciated the most to have done around the house when he got home. Were there some things that bothered him more than other things? His response floored me. "I really just like the counters clear and knowing there's a plan for dinner," he said. What?! I'd been killing myself on things that weren't all that important to him. Why had we never taken the time to figure out what our household priorities were? (Personally, I like clean floors and toilets.) Granted, we both love having the whole house clean and tidy. But I can't tell you how much easier things got in our home after that conversation. When I wasn't able to get to all the things I wanted to get done, I could just focus on what was most important to both of us.

You can too!

YOU'VE GOT THIS!

I encourage you to take some time to figure out your family priorities and your household priorities. If you're married, do this with your spouse to make sure you are both on the same page. What are all the various things you are trying to juggle right now? What might you be able to say no to in order to say yes to what's more important in your life—including time to get on top of the daily mayhem (and stress) that ensues in a home with kids? If you want your home to run efficiently, you have to create space for what's most important—both in your life and in your home. Knowing your family's priorities helps you do just that.

Unlocking Joy

Put some thought into answering these questions. They will help you prioritize all that you have going on. And remember, you might need to reevaluate some of these things down the road. That's normal. Life changes.

1. **Write down your "why."** Why do you want to get organized in your home?

   _____

   _____

   _____

2. **What are your family priorities?** Use the 4Fs to help you figure out where people, activities, and commitments in your life fit in with your priorities.

   Faith: _____

   Family: _____

   Friends: _____

   Fellow man: _____

   Other: _____

3. **What are your top "household" priorities?** Pick two or three home management tasks you'd like to see done consistently in your home (and ask your spouse too, if you are married).

_____

_____

_____

4. **What are a few things you can say no to right now in order to create more breathing room for you and your family?**

_____

_____

_____

Rule #3: Take Baby Steps

Slow and Steady for the Win

Moms are familiar with the wobbly first steps of their little ones. Learning how to walk takes time. Learning how to organize is not so different. To find success in our home management, we must simplify the projects and tasks we tackle and learn how to take "baby steps."

I don't know about you, but I tend to jump headfirst into a project and then get distracted and start another. As a consequence, I end up with several partially completed projects all around the house. I like to call this problem "Homemaking ADD." I might start a task downstairs but then realize I need something upstairs to help me finish it. However, once I'm upstairs I notice something else that needs my attention. It's not until I go back downstairs to get something for my new project that I remember why I went upstairs in the first place. It's a bit crazy, I know. My attention span just isn't what it should be, especially when I'm juggling too many to-dos in my head. (I know I'm not alone in this, though.) Needless to say, as the following story illustrates, I am the queen of breaking my own "baby steps" rule.

My "Little Red Wagon"

Years ago, my wonderful in-laws offered to watch Grant and Blake overnight when Steve and I were going to a business dinner with two executives from his company. This meant that I suddenly had two full days with no kids in the house. I was thrilled. I planned to get a ton of things done that I'd been putting off.

This is where I need to let you know that I am not only a visual learner but also a visual organizer. I need to see everything out to sort it and identify the best place for it to go. This is a great way to organize if you don't take on too many areas of your house at once. Sorting things before they get put away is vital, albeit a bit messy. So away I went, emptying drawers and closets and just about everything I could think of, sorting things into piles all over the floor, both upstairs and downstairs. I was in organizational bliss.

I had to stop my sorting to take a shower and get ready for our fancy dinner. (Really, it was just dinner at a nice restaurant. But I wasn't cooking and was going out with people taller than my kneecaps, which in my book is fancy.)

I'd been expecting Steve to call to let me know when he was going to be picking me up. However, when he did call he said something I had not expected.

"Hey, honey! I'm on my way. We decided to take one car to dinner, so I have everyone in the car with me—and they all want to see the house."

Silence. I was too stunned to say anything. Most of our house was torn apart. A complete mess.

"Kristi?"

I finally managed a response. "Okay, so how long do I have until you get here? Can you take any long ways home to buy me more time?"

He went on to tell me that they were about twenty minutes away. We'd been married long enough for him to understand my style of organizing, and he knew it was a natural disaster at home. I knew he was panicking as much as I was.

I hung up the phone, wondering how in the world I was going to get everything put away and, more importantly, not undo all the progress I had made. Most things were in piles ready to be put away, but there was no way to get it all done in only twenty minutes.

Enter my brilliant idea. The boys' little red wagon! I knew just where it was. Now, I should clarify that we called it our "little red wagon," but it was actually a huge wagon with large all-terrain tires. I ran downstairs and wheeled that baby throughout the house, stacking all those piles neatly inside of it. I stuck many piles carefully into brown grocery bags and labeled them with a permanent marker. Several trips to and from the garage with my wagon, and most of the mess was tucked away. Upstairs, I hid a few piles in closets. Not only was I able to just wheel my wagon into the garage and out of sight but the next day I was also able to wheel it around the house as I put things away. Mobile organization!

I finished tidying up just in time to put on some lipstick and answer the door. Talk about biting off more than I could chew!

The Antidote to Homemaking ADD: The Master List

Don't you sometimes wish you could just snap your fingers and have everything magically cleaned up and organized? Where is Mary Poppins when you need her? Often when I'm right in the middle of reorganizing a room, cupboard, or closet, someone inevitably "needs" me and I'm called away from my endeavor. This, of course, often leaves things in a worse state than before I started—half-done and a mess.

As much as it would be amazing to have Mary Poppins come and tidy our houses, there is a little magic we can muster up ourselves: **the magic of a master list!** I'm a list girl. I love my lists. However, that is sometimes the problem. I have too many to-do lists floating around, and my home organization to-dos get lost in the shuffle.

What I've learned through the years is that when it comes to getting the whole house organized, it's best for me to start by creating one "home organization" master list. This master list is where I record, room by room, all the small tasks and big projects I need to do. Keeping all the household organization tasks in one spot—on the master list—helps me focus on what needs to get done next instead of taking on tasks as I see them or trying to do too many projects at once.

In the rest of this chapter, I'm going to show you how to create (and organize) a home organization master list, as well as walk you through how to prioritize tasks and break down large projects into baby steps.

Steps for Creating a Home Organization Master List

Let's start at ground zero so you can understand how this master list works. Essentially, you'll be creating a master list, room by room and area by area, for the entire house. This master list will have a combination of all the decluttering and cleaning tasks you want to do and all the problems or challenges you want to address.

Here's a quick summary of the steps involved in creating a master list:

1. **Give each room or area its own page.** This is key, as it allows you to easily find tasks and add new to-dos as you identify them. Even if you only have a few tasks for a room or area, it's still helpful to start a new page. Don't be surprised if some rooms require several pages, such as the kitchen or garage. Write your tasks on the left-hand side

of each page and try to save some room on the right-hand side. I'll explain why a bit later.

2. **Designate a place to keep your master list.** Because it is going to contain multiple pages, I suggest keeping your master list in a small binder, notebook, journal, clipboard, or even a digital notebook like OneNote or Evernote. Keep your list where you can easily access it and not lose any part of it. I have printouts available to download (details at the end of the chapter) that you can use as a guideline for how to format your master list. Of course, you should feel free to adapt your list-making however you'd like.

3. **Think about the possibilities.** Now, don't laugh, but one of the things I do when creating a master list is to pray for a vision for each room. I try to envision the best function for each room. I ask God to give me a little extra inspiration as to how I can best use the room to be a blessing to my family and others who enter my home. There may be some creative ways to add more seating to a room or storage to an area that I hadn't originally thought of before. What do I need that room to do? What things should I get rid of or buy to maximize the functionality of that room? As new ideas come to mind, I add them to my list and think of any aspects of the project that might require a few baby steps.

Get Walking

Now it's time to walk through your house and write down all the tasks you want and need to get done in each room. Don't forget to start a new page whenever you switch rooms. Go slowly, room by room, making a detailed list. Remember to make a list for areas that tend to collect clutter, like bathrooms, closets, entry areas, the pantry, hallways, and stairs. If you are married, I encourage you to do your walk-through with your spouse. Sometimes it takes two sets of eyes to see what needs to get done. Often something that doesn't bother you might bother your spouse, and they will appreciate that task making the list.

As you walk through each room, keep in mind:

> Any problems or issues you're having in that room that you want to address (like how to get rid of the paper piles constantly collecting on the counter).
> Any repairs needed (like a broken cupboard door).
> Any items you need to purchase in order to make the area more organized (like new drawer organizers or baskets for shelves).
> Any ideas for remodeling or decorating needs (like adding a new bookcase for your growing collection of books).
> Any items that need to go or be replaced (like an old broken chair).

To get you started, here are a few examples of items that might end up on your master list. (Okay, I'll be honest. A few of these tasks have been on my own master list.)

Master Bedroom Tasks

> Organize the master closet
> Clear out boxes under the bed
> Put away laundry piled on the bedroom chair

> Wipe down baseboards
> Get a new dresser with better storage
> Wash comforter and mattress cover

Bathroom Tasks

> Clean out the cupboard under the sink
> Declutter all drawers and cupboards
> Re-caulk shower and bathtub

> Unclog sink
> Figure out better storage for items on the counter
> Clean grout

Kitchen Tasks

> Fix leaking sink faucet
> Put cupboard door back on
> Wipe down floorboards
> Wipe down cupboards and walls

> Clear piles off the counter
> Figure out a solution for incoming mail and coupons

Family Room Tasks

> Figure out better toy storage
> Add putting pajamas away to the kids' morning chore list
> Polish side tables (and fill in scratches)

> Create a better solution for the collection of socks and shoes scattered around
> Sort through magazines
> Organize DVDs

At this point, you are a bit like a detective. You are trying to uncover problem areas and the main to-dos throughout your house. Eventually, we'll identify systems you may need to implement. For instance, those clothes that always end up piled on the chair in the bedroom may be an indicator that you need a better laundry system. If toys are constantly strewn around the family room, you may need better toy management systems or chore systems. You don't need to come up with solutions at this point in the process (we'll get to that in phase II). When creating your master list the focus is twofold: first identifying tasks that need to get done and then identifying the problems (or problem areas) you need solved.

Instead of attempting several items on the list at once, tackle your master list one project at a time—and one step at a time. This is how to create doable, bite-sized projects that you will actually complete. It's difficult to declutter and organize every room and area of your house in a day or even two days, but you may be able to finish most of your to-dos in a smaller area, like a hall closet, in a day. You could declutter and organize one section of a room or one cupboard or drawer fairly quickly. By creating a master list, you can see exactly what needs to get done and intentionally choose tasks that you can easily finish with the time you have. No more Homemaking ADD.

Prioritizing the Items on Your Master List

Once you've created your master list, it's time to prioritize the items, beginning with which room to tackle first. If you can't decide which room you want to start in, you can simply look over your master list and rank each room in order of importance using my little ABC scale:

A = Absolutely needs to get done soon

B = Better get done soon

C = Can wait to be done later

After you have decided which room to start decluttering and organizing, you can begin applying the ABC scale to each task for that room. Use the margin area on the left-hand side of your list pages to write your ABCs. If you notice a task that is a little more involved and would make a great project, then add a little *P* next to it too.

Be honest with yourself when sorting the items on your list into these three ABC categories. It's easy to think some projects are more urgent than they really are. As much as cleaning out the hall closet may feel like something that has to get done immediately, I'd suggest focusing your attention on areas of the house that impact the day-to-day function of your home. For instance, messy counters are more visible than messy drawers, so I would give decluttering my counters an *A* and my utensil drawer a *C*, because a neat utensil drawer isn't vital to the daily flow of the house. As long as the utensils are clean, that's good enough for now. The bottom line is this: **you need to properly categorize in order to organize!** You need to know what things on your list need your attention first.

Slow and Steady!

Once you have at least one room prioritized, choose one task to begin working on. Remember that attempting to multitask is not usually a home organizer's best friend. If the task is small and easy to complete, then just get it done and check it off.

Keep in mind that some tasks may need to become a project, with its own dedicated page of detailed baby steps for getting it done. The beautiful thing about tackling a project in bite-sized pieces is that you can accomplish it little by little until the project is complete.

For example, organizing large spaces like the garage can be a huge project that requires multiple steps, so I typically give the garage its own page right off the bat and break each task down into baby steps. Sometimes there are more steps to cleaning out our garage and sometimes there are fewer, but here's a sampling of the tasks that have appeared on my garage list.

Garage Tasks

> Empty the garage completely and declutter
> Sweep floor and knock down cobwebs
> Throw away all old boxes and any other trash
> Take donation items to Salvation Army
> Text friends pictures of items I think they might want (like things my kids have outgrown)
> Take pictures and post items I want to sell (and put them back in the garage last so I can easily access them)
> Buy storage shelves and bins
> Redistribute items that belong in the house
> Sort things to be stored into bins and label clearly
> Figure out the best way to store bins that don't fit on the storage shelves

Strategize Solutions

Regardless of the size of the task, another important element to getting and keeping our house organized is to strategize solutions to the issues in each room. First we determine the cause of the problem and then we brainstorm potential solutions. As I'm researching or thinking through ideas for how to address a problem area, I use the reserved right-hand side of the list pages to write down items I might need to buy or solutions I've come up with.

TOOLBOX TIP

I always completely empty the garage when I'm cleaning it out. I sort things as I take them out of the garage, so I'm not having to move things twice. (I use the decluttering systems detailed in chapter 12 to categorize my piles.)

Sometimes coming up with the solution is easier than we might think. For instance, once I figured out that the reason my three youngest kiddos kept leaving their sweatshirts on the floor was that they couldn't reach the hangers or the rod in the hall closet, I quickly came up with a solution. I ordered some hooks for the back of the closet door and stuck them low enough for my kids to reach. Next, I showed them where their new hooks were and how I wanted them to hang up their sweatshirts. Then I had them practice hanging up their sweatshirts so they wouldn't fall off the hooks. Problem solved . . . well, they still forget from time to time. So we practice again.

YOU'VE GOT THIS!

Organizing requires a certain amount of self-control—like not trying to take on too much at a time. Make a master list, room by room and area by area, and list out all the steps you need to take to organize that space. Prioritize what you want to get done and what's most pressing, then show yourself grace as you work through your tasks step by step. Work slowly and steadily. Don't kill yourself trying to do too much at once. Just think how good it will feel to check those items off your list as you get them done.

Unlocking Joy

Your master list is the starting point for bringing order to your home. Slowly work through these steps and you'll see the joy start emerging as you finally get things done.

1. **Create your master list.** Figure out if you are going to create your list digitally or on paper. Then start going room by room, making your list. Be sure to organize your list by room, writing

57

the name of each room at the top of the page. Remember to use a new page for each room, so you can add more room-related tasks if needed. You can access my printables for creating a master list at: **KristiClover.com/MOMPrintables**. Also, decide how you will store your master list. I highly recommend a small half-inch binder or a clipboard.

☐ I will use paper   ☐ I will go with a digital list

☐ I finished making my master list!

* Now do a little dance! This is your first big step in tackling your mayhem!

2. **Prioritize your list.** First, prioritize your rooms using the ABC method. Choose which room you will tackle first. Which room will you be starting with?

_____

_____

3. **Now prioritize the tasks in this room and pick one project to start working on.** What are some of the "baby steps" that this project can be broken down into?

_____

_____

_____

Rule #4: Do Your "Worst Thing" First!

Attacking the Projects We Tend to Put Off

Almost two years ago, our family did something unexpected that required us to clean and organize our house from top to bottom—including the garage. A dear friend of mine was in a difficult season and couldn't find an affordable place for her and her children to live. Steve and I prayed about it, talked it over with the kids, and ended up inviting them to move in with us. Now, keep in mind that we are a family of seven. My friend also had five kids, which means we had *ten kids* living in our house—for almost six months.

Our whole family went to work cleaning and decluttering every room in preparation for their arrival. Even my little girls got involved in the process, since they were giving up their room and needed to move their toys and clothes out. We doubled up kids in rooms, used air mattresses, turned couches into beds, and shoved dressers and bins into corners. We even cleaned out the garage and made several Salvation Army runs in order to make room for them to store things. We made it work. It was incredible to see just how motivated we all were to get projects that had long been put off finished so quickly.

As you can imagine, having that many people living under one roof was challenging at times, but overall it turned out to be a great experience. We were able to get most of the house organized before they moved in, the chores charts were updated, and meal planning was figured out regularly. We had lots of parent meetings to tweak schedules and rules, but their time with us was pretty smooth and was actually a ton of fun. We joked that it was like a nonstop family camp. Every meal was a party. And if the kids had their way, every night would have been a movie night.

But here's the question: How do we motivate ourselves to take on those big, daunting projects when we don't have a deadline—no houseguests coming, no holiday dinner, no party to host? Those are usually the types of things that light a fire under us to get on top of projects we've been neglecting. Well, the not-so-easy answer is that we have to look at what we've been ignoring and figure out why we've been ignoring it.

What's Your "Worst Thing"?

Determining what those neglected tasks are isn't all that difficult. If you created your own master task list in the last chapter, then you probably noticed that you wrote down a few things that seem to constantly show up on your to-do lists. We all have them. Those items we tend to put off. Those things that nag at us month after month and move from one to-do list to the next. I consider these tasks our "worst things." They may even be the tasks on your master list that you quickly categorized as a C item. You may have even wondered if there was a D for "Don't even think I'll ever do this!" We usually have a reason for our procrastination. Sometimes we think the project will take too long; other times we just don't like the work involved in getting it done. Whatever the reason, these overwhelming tasks never seem to become a priority—and the work is left undone. But through the years I've discovered that freedom and a deep sense of accomplishment come when I take the time to conquer the projects that plague me.

My "worst thing" has been getting our digital photos organized and printed through the years. More specifically, getting photos into albums or onto walls. I love taking photos, but since we went digital, my photos just sit on my phone and computer. I'm horrible. I know. I did two big photo album catch-up projects and had most of our family pictures in albums up to the year that Wade (#3) was born. Not great, but I'd been making a dent. However, since I started blogging, which was the year after Caitlyn (#5) was born, the number of photos and videos I take has skyrocketed and I've gotten behind again.

Now, before you think I'm a complete slacker for getting behind on my photos yet again, keep in mind that many of the projects we completed before our friends moved in had been on my "worst things" list. Organizing our photos wasn't a priority for making our home more functional . . . until the day when my girls mentioned that they weren't in any of our family albums. (Oh, the guilt!) My poor girls had no printed photos of themselves other than the few I'd had framed.

Eat the Frog!

You may think I'm crazy for suggesting that you make at least one big "worst thing" on your master list an A-level priority. But I don't want you to be tormented by that persistently skipped "worst thing" anymore. Besides, you already know a few basics about how to get projects done. You make a list and break it down. That's always the starting point. In this chapter, I'm going to show you how to create a plan of attack for these sidelined obstacles. I know exactly how good it has felt to get items like this off my lists, and I want you to experience that same feeling: *victory*! **I also want you to see that there is no task too big or scary to take on.** What I'm getting at is best described by this famous quote, credited to Mark Twain: "Eat a live frog first thing in the morning and nothing worse will happen to you the rest of the day." In other words, **confronting the hard things makes everything else easier.** There's wisdom in those words!

Creating a Plan of Attack

When we create a plan of attack, we must look for ways to set ourselves up for success. This is where we circle back to prioritizing our days. You may need to clear your schedule a bit in order to devote some time to get this particular project done. Yes, you could just do one baby step at a time, little by little working your way through the project task list. But I want you to know how to efficiently get large projects done. So let's attack this "worst thing" head-on.

Pick Your Worst "Worst Thing" to Conquer

You may know exactly what your "worst thing" is. If that's the case, great. However, humor me for a moment and do something fun. Pull out your master list and look it over room by room. Regardless of what level of priority you have given each task or project, I want you to circle two or three things in each room that drive you crazy. While you may circle some A items, it's more likely that you will circle a few items in the C category, because we tend to avoid doing things we dislike. Common "worst things" are cleaning out the garage, organizing photos, sorting bins that have been stored away for a long time, household DIY projects, decluttering file cabinets, cleaning out pantries and freezers, and so much more.

One thing to consider when you are deciding which "worst thing" to tackle first is whether your master list includes tasks that are "hidden" because they are digital in nature, such as organizing the files on your computer, downloading photos and videos from your phone to your computer, and more. Take a moment to identify any projects that you may not have included on your master list because they fall outside of your typical household tasks and write them down. You can label the page "Digital Tasks" or "Miscellaneous Tasks." Then look over all the tasks that drive you crazy and pick your least-favorite thing—your worst "worst thing." Make it a good one. I'm telling you, it's going to feel great to take it off your list.

Once you've identified your "worst thing," it's time to create some realistic steps for how to tackle it. We'll use mine—photos—as an example of how to do this.

Schedule a Time for Tackling This Project

The first time I organized our photos, I called in reinforcements. I asked my in-laws to take the kids for a couple of days. I put those dates on my calendar and planned out my two days. If having your kids stay with family or friends is not a realistic option for you, you may need to get creative. Perhaps you could work on your project during nap times, or maybe you could ask a friend to watch your kids for a few hours (or for the day if possible). Just put your "day of battle" on the calendar—and don't flake. You owe it to yourself to stick to this and see it through. You may even want to create some peer pressure and tell someone about your plan, or mention it on social media. You might even enlist help from a friend or from your kids.

Work Backward

Start with the end in mind. What are you trying to accomplish? Something like "organize my closet" is pretty vague. Be specific. **Think through how you want your project to look in the end—and be realistic.** Questions to consider are:

> What do you want your closet to look like?
> Do you need to get rid of older clothes or just organize what you have?
> Do you need to purchase anything to create the feel for this area that you're going for, such as a bench to sit on while getting ready?
> Will you store your jewelry in your closet or elsewhere?
> Do you need more storage for what you plan to keep in here?

Ask yourself enough questions to figure out what your end goal will look like.

The first time I tackled our photos, I originally wanted to create scrapbooks. However, this would have taken me months to finish, and I only had two days. By working backward I realized that my primary goal was to pick my favorite photos, get them printed, and put them into albums or frames to be displayed around the house. So that is what I focused on. I figured I could always scrapbook them some other time.

Create a List of Supplies You Will Need

In the case of my photo project, I had to buy albums, frames, and nails for hanging some of the frames. Getting the frames in advance helped me to know what size photos to print.

Of course, not every task requires supplies. However, even organizing the garage may require a few new bins, some large bags for trash and donations, and possibly some hooks for hanging things. Be sure to buy or order what you will need *before* your scheduled project day.

Break Things Down into Bite-Sized Tasks

Plan out your day. Ask yourself, *What will I do first, and what are all the things that need to be done?* In my case, I knew I needed to sort the digital photos on my computer, select and tag my favorites, send them off to be printed, pick them up, and then put them into albums or frames. I was also printing photos to share with family members, so I made a list of who needed which photos and then sorted the prints into piles to be mailed.

Eliminate Distractions

It's easy to get distracted when working on a project. As you know, I struggle with this. Hunger is a big distraction for me. When I'm working on a project, I try to make sure I have easy meals and snacks I can grab and keep working. (Okay, so maybe I stock some of my favorite ice cream in the freezer to celebrate my diligence for the day!) Because I know I can get distracted when I walk around the house, I make myself stay in one area to limit the temptation to do something else. At times I've even let a friend know what I'm doing and asked her to check up on me—just not during my work time.

Get It Done!

You can do it! You will be so grateful that you took the time and energy to work on this big project and get it done. The completion of this "worst thing" project will act as a catalyst for you to jump in and get other projects off your big list.

YOU'VE GOT THIS!

Going into home organization with a "game plan" is always the best strategy—and the most efficient way for getting things done. Now you have a detailed approach for how to attack even your least-favorite projects, and you don't have to be afraid of any task on your list. You can conquer anything. **You are a chaos conqueror!** Take on that "worst thing" and finally get it off your to-do list.

Unlocking Joy

1. **What is your "worst thing"?** Take a look at your master list and pick one "worst thing" from the tasks you circled that you'd like to finally get off your to-do list.

   _____

   _____

   _____

2. **Create your battle plan for conquering your "worst thing."**
   When will you do it?

   _____

   What will that project look like done?

   _____

   What supplies will you need?

   _____

   What are the specific bite-sized action steps?

   _____

   _____

   _____

   _____

What distractions do you foresee?

_____

_____

_____

_____

Rule #5: Clear the Clutter

Rethinking Our Relationship with "Stuff"

In early 2018 my grandma had a second recurrence of cancer, and her doctors told her they were out of treatment options. The time had come for us to pack up the car and drive our family up to central Oregon to see her for our final goodbyes.

Before we arrived, my uncle warned me repeatedly about how bad things were, but he wasn't talking about my grandmother's health. I knew just how serious her cancer was. He was referring to her mobile home. My grandma had become quite a hoarder. Again, I knew this, but my uncle still felt the need to warn me.

Grandma had actually been quite organized when I was growing up. In fact, I developed my love for labeling from her. She owned the first label maker I'd ever seen. Everything in her home was labeled. Not only did she put her photos into albums but she also wrote the date and detailed information on the back of *every* photo. Oh, if only I'd learned that habit from her! There was no denying Grandma was organized.

But she refused to throw anything away. She had been a book-keeper for years and had saved everything—and I truly mean *everything*. Old files that had no purpose, old mail, old magazine clippings, appliance manuals, receipts, broken baskets, travel bags, sewing and crocheting supplies, used resealable plastic bags, broken kitchen items, outdated food, books—oh, the books! My grandma was an avid reader and could have opened a library. You get the point. She saved everything.

My family loved the time we spent with Grandma that last visit. She slept on and off, since her pain medication made her drowsy. Every moment I saw that she was occupied with the kids or starting to doze off, I'd jump up and try to clean and declutter a few areas. I wanted her to have a cleaner, healthier environment. But I also wanted to be respectful. She didn't like anything moved or changed. So I'd clean up, then take her the box of things I'd deemed unnecessary in that space and ask if I could put them on an upper shelf in her hallway. Somehow, she said yes more than no to this suggestion. My dad and uncle couldn't believe she was letting me move things. She'd never allowed them to touch anything because they'd threatened to throw everything away, and she was afraid they would get rid of something she viewed as valuable. But my approach didn't seem to bother her. Plus, we shared a special bond, and she trusted me to know what was important to her.

After our final goodbyes and prayers, we made the long journey home. Grandma passed away less than two months later. She was a fighter. She held out as long as she could. We had lots of great conversations leading up to her final day. I will always treasure my memories of my grandma. She was fun and always knew how to spoil a grandkid—and she made the world's best tuna melts and clam dip.

The week after she passed, my oldest son and I flew out to attend the funeral and to help my uncle get her mobile home ready to sell. My grandma's ability to organize had enabled her to maximize every square inch of space. There was stuff everywhere. So much stuff. Lots and lots of stuff. The guest room was so full of stuff we could barely open the door. It took the three of us a full day to find and unbury the bed! It was overwhelming. Let's just say that a knack for organizing and a tendency to hoard are a horrible combination for a family to contend with after a loved one passes away.

Dealing with Clutter

Despite what some professional organizers might tell you, there is such a thing as organized clutter. My grandma is the perfect example of someone who "organized clutter" for far too long. While she was an extreme example, many of us often save and store things that should be tossed out or given a new home (preferably someone else's). Whether it is tucking things away into baskets or displaying too many trinkets on shelves, it's easy to continue storing our clutter and "organizing" it rather than periodically taking stock of all we have. I've been known to throw things in a bin and stick a label on it, knowing that it's clutter I'm just not ready to sort through. It may make me feel better for the moment because things are put away and out of sight, but it's just organized clutter that needs to be dealt with.

Decluttering is definitely one of the most important parts of the organizational process. It is such a big topic that I've divided it into two chapters. These two chapters may just be the most important ones for you to implement. In chapter 12, "Decluttering Systems," I'll cover some tips and techniques for tackling clutter and offer some creative solutions for tough-to-conquer problem areas. My goal in *this* chapter is to help you to better understand why you might be struggling with clutter and to help you rethink your relationship with your stuff.

Why We Struggle with Clutter

Family Life Often Requires More Stuff

The moment Steve and I brought our first child home we embarked on the crazy train of acquiring more stuff, aka clutter. Like most first-time parents, we stocked up on everything we thought we'd need for our new little one. As the years went by—and as more kids were added to the mix—we acquired more and more possessions and paraphernalia: school projects, photos, artwork, clothes of various sizes, and more. Families like ours always have a need to declutter along the way. Life gets busy, and when we don't periodically slow down enough to deal with all that's accumulating, we're left with a large decluttering project.

> When a home is cluttered, it creates stress and chaos—and nothing brings about more clutter than a growing family.

The Lack of a Designated Storage Space

Remember the quote at the beginning of this book? "A place for everything, and everything in its place." I love it because it is so true. Everything in your house needs a "home." In fact, **I believe one of the primary causes of clutter is the lack of designated storage spaces for items.** Often we have things sitting on our counters and piled in corners because we've never taken the time to designate a spot to put them. So, as you start decluttering, look for these "homeless items" in your home. Take the time to create a file, find a container, or simply assign those items a drawer to go in. **If it's important enough to keep, then it's**

> ### TOOLBOX TIP
>
> When giving items new "homes" throughout your living space, don't forget to give them an "address" too. A label is like a street address, providing the precise location for your article's new home. Labels help everyone remember where to locate your newly organized things throughout your home.

important enough to create a space for. Otherwise, these items will just find themselves at home in a pile on your counter again.

When choosing a new location for something, Dana White has a great tip from her book *Decluttering at the Speed of Life*. She suggests asking yourself, *If I were looking for this item, where would I look first?** I love that. I often lose track of things when I put them in "creative" spots. Instead, take Dana's advice and ask yourself where you or your family members would logically look for the item. I used to misplace my sunglasses all the time. I was constantly having to retrace my steps to figure out where I'd put them. My husband advised me to set them down in only one or two places. I chose my purse (their true home) and on the counter next to my cell phone. Having a designated home for my sunglasses worked, and now I rarely lose them.

Not Taking the Time to Put Things Away

If you aren't taking the time to actually do the work of putting things away, it doesn't matter if you have a "home" for everything or all kinds of wonderful systems to make your family life run smoothly. Until you actually put things away, clutter will just continue to accumulate. Now, I understand that you may not be the culprit behind the reappearing piles. I sometimes feel totally defeated at the end of the day when I discover that my kids have

---

*Dana White, *Decluttering at the Speed of Life: Winning Your Never-Ending Battle with Stuff* (Nashville: W Publishing Group, 2018), 63.

been playing in several rooms of the house and never took the time to pick up after themselves. This is where the next chapter on habit training and routines (for you and your family) will come into play, as well as some helpful chore systems.

Overvaluing Our "Stuff"

It's easy to overvalue our possessions, whether for monetary or sentimental reasons. This is another reason why many people have so much clutter and was probably one of the biggest reasons for my grandma's clutter. She hated to throw away outdated food or items that were damaged. She had spent money on those items and felt it was not financially responsible to just get rid of them. Same with items that she never used but thought she might find a purpose for someday. When she tried to sell things in a garage sale, she would price her treasures just below the amount she'd spent on them. Of course, this meant the garage was packed with stuff that never sold.

Not only do we hold on to things too long because of the money we spent on them but we also do it because of their sentimental value to us. Through the years, I've saved mementos, ticket stubs, letters, love notes, maps from places we've been, church crafts, coloring pages, noodle art, clay creations, doodles, and more. I used to tell myself, *Someday I'll put these in a scrapbook,* or *No good mommy throws away any love note or personalized drawings.* Right? So I'd throw it all in a bin, put on a pretty

TOOLBOX TIP

If I buy something and don't end up using it, I just see if a friend might like it. This takes my focus off the money I spent and helps me feel like I was able to bless a friend that day. I know I've enjoyed the hand-me-downs given to us through the years, so why not return the favor?

label, and stick my box of "treasures" in the back of a deep closet. Problem is, most of it was simply organized clutter.

Emotions can often cloud our judgment. Sorting through the bins I brought home from my grandma's home was hard. Although I'd tried to pack only the most important things I wanted to keep, I still ended up "inheriting" more than I needed. Each and every bin I opened was filled with memories. Afghans she crocheted (many that had won first prize at the state fair), kitchen tools (that I remember using right alongside her as a child), costume jewelry (that had no real value but I remembered her wearing), and so much more. I had all kinds of emotional attachments to her things. Okay, yes, I guess you could say that I was attached to her clutter. I kept that in my mind as I went through those bins.

There are plenty of things that are fine to store. However, it's easy to store items we just haven't gotten rid of yet—or because we overvalue them for financial or nostalgic reasons. Be sure to check out my tips for storing sentimental keepsakes in chapter 14, "Storage Systems."

Rethinking Our Relationship with Our Stuff

Years ago something happened that changed my perspective on what is truly important and had a huge impact on how I view all our possessions.

San Diego is often plagued with wildfires, and one year, shortly after learning that we were pregnant with our third child, there was a huge wildfire heading straight for our house. The hurricane-force winds whipped through the canyon behind our home and the surrounding areas, making it impossible for firefighters to contain the fire. The news showed maps of affected areas and areas that would most likely be devoured by the flames in the oncoming days. The winds were not forecast to die down for three days—and the maps showed that the fire would be in our neighborhood on day two.

All that first day we kept a close eye on the news and began to pack up a few things in case of evacuation. At the time we still had Daisy, our seventy-pound Rhodesian Ridgeback. So dog food and space for her in the minivan had to be taken into account. I took a quick video of every square inch of our house to ensure that our insurance company would have an accurate account if we did lose the house. My priorities were crystal clear that night. If we got out of the house with nothing more than our children and our dog, I would be happy. Sure, I would be bummed too. But at that moment, our safety was of utmost importance.

Since we did have several hours to prepare before the call came to evacuate, I had time to grab a few things. You know what I grabbed? It wasn't the bins of baby clothes or the art portfolios, or even my grandma's china. I grabbed our computers, backup hard drives, photos that weren't on our hard drive and the negatives from our wedding photos, cell phones and chargers, important documents, a few photos from the wall, my jewelry box (which I later realized was silly, because I really wear only costume jewelry), a small bag of clothes for each of us, two of my boys' favorite stuffed animals and a few toys (mainly to keep them occupied in the hotel), snacks, water, dog food, and, finally, a leash. That is what I was able to cram into our minivan.

We left as the sun was just beginning to come up over the hills. It was eerie and red from the smoke. We said goodbye to our home and drove away. The smoke was so heavy going north that we ended up turning around and staying downtown in the city. Later that day I told Grant and Blake that we'd probably never see our house again. Grant was immediately concerned about his toys and other stuffed animals. "Toys and everything else in the house can be replaced. We can always buy new furniture and dishes, but we can't ever get a new you," I explained as I hugged him tight. I felt myself relax and exhale, knowing in my heart I truly believed this.

By a miracle, the winds died down a day earlier than expected. The fire came right up to the canyon behind our house. Neighbors who stayed behind longer than we did said they saw the tall flames coming closer and closer, but the incredible heroes within the fire department were able to get the fire contained. We were the lucky ones that year. Many other families lost their homes, including one of the newscasters who we'd been watching all night. My heart sank for all those who lost so much.

In the hours I had to pack up, I was forced to rethink my relationship with everything we had in our home. The monetary and sentimental values that I thought everything had just weren't as important as I'd believed. Since then I've learned to hold more loosely to things and not be as bothered when items are broken or lost in our home. Decluttering has also gotten a lot easier.

You know the joke that you never see a moving van behind a hearse? Well, it's true. After experiencing the fire evacuation and losing my grandma, I gained a much better perspective on what I should allow to remain in my home. The more I declutter now, the bigger the blessing I will leave for my kids, who won't have to riffle through all of my worldly possessions after I'm gone. Plus, it's a blessing for the here and now. A clutter-free home feels so good!

YOU'VE GOT THIS!

Determining what is clutter and what to do with it can be exhausting work. It takes time and energy—both physical and mental—to declutter well. Putting things out of sight and out of mind is not the solution. Don't hide the mess or avoid dealing with it by organizing it into a cute little bin or basket. Deal with it. As you begin to sort through your belongings, ask yourself how important each item in your home *really* is—and keep only what's best and useful. We're going to get extremely practical about the best ways to declutter in the second section of this book. For now, take time to think through problem areas where clutter is gathering and start assigning new homes for things that truly belong in your space.

Unlocking Joy

1. Do you have any hoarding habits? If so, what are they?

_____

_____

_____

2. Where does your clutter tend to hide and accumulate?

_____

_____

_____

3. What would you grab if you were being evacuated from your home? What would you miss the most? Do you even know where those things are, if you had to grab them in an emergency?

_____

_____

_____

Rule #6: Get Your Groove On

The Power of Routines and Habits

We frequently have family dance parties in our home as a way to tire out the kids at the end of the night. We all love to dance—freestyle. I always thought I could be an amazing dancer, and early in our marriage, I decided it'd be fun to take a ballroom dancing class. I had a coupon, and Steve and I were overdue for a date night. I'd never done any formal dancing other than the swaying back and forth thing at dances in junior high and high school. But it took only one class for me to discover something I'd never known before: I have two left feet! I was totally embarrassed. Steve, on the other hand, turned out to be a really good dancer. He took cotillion classes in school and still remembered all the steps.

He was so patient with me as he tried to explain the box step. Yes, I struggled with the box step. I understood the whole "box" element of it. What threw me was which foot moved forward and which foot moved backward at the corners of our box.

Granted, I'm sure I could improve with time and practice, so maybe my dreams of winning *Dancing with the Stars* don't have to be shattered.

Nor do your dreams of getting organized. Organization is an art that takes time and practice to master. It also doesn't matter how great you *think* you are at it. It's not until you actually *do* the hard work of creating order over and over again that you master the steps and get your groove on. As I said earlier: our goal of getting more organized is learning to be *more efficient* in our home—not more perfect. **Creating efficiency in our home is all about finding the right rhythm so that our family can productively perform the tasks, chores, and routines that need to be done regularly.** If we don't, we will continue to do things the hard way (and possibly step on some toes in the process).

The Beauty of Routines and Habits

Most moms keep a rather long to-do list in their heads.

> Go grocery shopping
> Figure out who needs to be where and when
> Find my cell phone
> Get the dishes into the dishwasher so there are clean dishes for dinner
> Put the laundry away and start the next load
> Plan what to make for dinner
> Find my cell phone again

The list goes on and on. Overwhelming, isn't it? How can we remember everything we need to do? If you are like me, you find that you can't. When I was pregnant there was a hormonal thing going on causing my brain fog. Now it's just everyday life that can leave me in a bit of a daze.

However, my inability to remember all the things I need to do has motivated me to slow down and take a look at what routines I could create in order to free up some space in my brain.

> When we create habits and routines for getting things done, the less we have to think through what has to get done and when to do things.

That's the beauty of habits. The more you do something, the more automatic it becomes. We're literally training our brain to switch to auto-pilot. When we turn everyday to-dos and weekly to-dos into routines, we form what I call "efficiency habits." Experience has taught me that the best way to create efficiency habits is to:

> Figure out the best time to get things done (which is the focus of this chapter).
> Prepare properly to complete our tasks (addressed in the next chapter).
> Do those tasks regularly (discussed in chapter 11).

Even if we have some bad habits, it's possible to replace them with efficiency habits. I know because this former "never made her bed" teen now makes her bed every day. I don't even think about it. I just get out of bed, pull my covers up, put the pretty pillows on, and voila! My bed is made. It's become a habit. ("Finally!" I hear my mom say in my head.) Some new habits might take longer to establish than others, but good routines performed consistently can break bad habits.

> While efficiency is the goal, consistency is the key to lasting organization.

81

Definitely Not a One-Size-Fits-All Thing

Sounds simple enough, right? Well, it can be simple, but first we need to remember that every family is different. As I pointed out earlier, few aspects of getting organized are truly a one-size-fits-all thing. The same is true when it comes to developing efficiency habits and routines.

You have to take a look at your family's schedule and needs first, then devise some routines and systems to put into place. If you're an early riser, you can probably get a few more things done in the morning than those who start their days later. My husband has an irregular travel schedule, so our routine varies from week to week, unlike families who have a more consistent (and reliable) weekly schedule. When Steve is in town, he works at home, and we usually eat dinner at 6:00 p.m. However, when he's out of town, the kids and I tend to eat dinner a bit earlier (mostly because I'm really tired by that time of the day and start bedtime routines earlier so the kids are all in bed on time). Our family fun night also gets moved around, depending on his travel schedule, versus being assigned a permanent day.

Regardless of what your family's schedule looks like, or the mix of ages and stages you have in your home, **the routines and habits you create need to be customized to fit your family's unique dynamics**. The better you construct your routines to work with the ebb and flow of your typical day, the better your routines will work to establish lasting habits.

Routine Tasks versus Master List Tasks

Before we dive in, I want to be sure you understand how your list of routine tasks differs from the tasks on your master list.

Master list tasks are usually room-related tasks you can cross off your list when they are done. Picking up shoes on the floor, folding a pile of laundry that's on top of the dryer, organizing the hall closet, and so on are all examples of tasks that will be part of your master list. However, the tasks that we'll create a routine for are those daily and weekly tasks and chores that need to get done repetitively, like doing dishes and laundry, brushing your teeth, taking a shower, getting dressed, putting on makeup, and making your bed. Typically, your routine tasks are not the same as those on your master list. But I will say that creating routines for your recurring tasks may just be the solution for some of those problems on your master list that need to be addressed, such as those toys that are always tossed about (tidying routine), clean clothes that always need to be put away (laundry routine), and dishes that endlessly stack up on the counter (chore routine).

Hopefully, the difference between your master list and your list of routines is clear. It's time to explore how to implement routines that will make your home more efficient.

Creating a Routine That Works Best for Your Family

In this section I'm going to walk you through the process I use to create a new routine for my family. Every new school year I reevaluate what we have going on for the year, what our days are going to look like, and what new or different tasks we need to get done throughout the week. As my kids get older the dynamics change. For example, some tasks that were once on my to-do list for the morning, like getting my little ones dressed, become tasks they can accomplish themselves.

There are a few key components involved in creating a great routine for your family:

> Know what tasks you and each family member need to get done every day and week.

> Assign daily tasks to certain times of the day.

> Assign weekly chores to certain days of the week.

Determine What Needs to Get Done: Daily and Weekly

When I sit down to figure out what routines I need to create, I first take an inventory of *everything* our family does each day and throughout the week. What do we need to get done every morning? What do we need to get done in the afternoon? What do we need to get done in the evening? Is there something that I'd like to start doing more regularly or have my kids do more regularly? I keep this list on the counter for several days, because it never fails that I initially forget a few things.

As I'm making this list, I jot down names or initials next to tasks that may be given to a particular person. I don't worry about truly assigning all the chores to individuals yet. Sometimes I'll write "all" or "kids" next to tasks. Since Steve's schedule is unpredictable, I don't include him into our daily and weekly routines. When he's home, he jumps in and helps wherever he's needed.

At this point in the process, all I care about is what tasks need to be completed daily (D) or weekly (W) and who might be responsible to complete that task. For example:

> Brushing teeth: daily / all
> Making the bed: daily / all
> Taking a shower: daily / all
> Practicing piano: daily / kids
> Putting away clean dishes: daily / assigned later
> Wiping down counters: daily / assigned later
> Packing lunches: daily / kids (even little kids can pack their own lunches)
> Doing laundry: weekly / all
> Meal planning and grocery shopping: weekly / me

Some tasks, such as taking out the kitchen trash, only need to get done once or twice a week. Many of our daily tasks are things we'll do every morning and every evening, such as brushing teeth and putting dishes in the dishwasher. I group our daily hygiene tasks into morning and bedtime routines. For instance:

Morning routine: Get up, get dressed, put pajamas in the hamper, flush toilet (yes, that's on our list), brush hair, wash face, eat breakfast, put dishes in dishwasher, brush teeth, do morning chores, and so on.

Evening routine: Do evening chores, get pajamas on, put dirty clothes in the hamper, go to the bathroom (flush!), brush and floss teeth, tidy room (this is probably considered a chore), read Bible together, and so on.

Until my kids get the hang of their morning and evening routines, I keep the list very detailed. I'll go into more detail on how to create checklists for your kids' morning and evening routines and how to set up chore systems in chapter 15.

Figure Out the Best Time to Do Specific Tasks

Now that you've identified *what* tasks need to get done, let's figure out *when* the best and most efficient time of the day is to get them done.

We had a dish dilemma in our home. It seemed like we never had clean dishes when we needed them. The dishwasher was always full of dirty dishes or midway through a cleaning cycle when it was dinnertime. In the hustle and bustle of our day, I consistently forgot to start the dishwasher. I also realized I loved mornings when I'd come downstairs to either an empty dishwasher or at least one full of clean dishes. Our days seemed to go much smoother in the dish department on those days. However, we didn't always fill our dishwasher every evening, so I didn't always turn it on.

Then one day it dawned on me: I didn't care about my internal "only run the dishwasher when it's full" rule. It was more important to me to have clean dishes every morning and to have a clear, dish-free counter every night. I'm such a rebel.

Maybe you have fewer people in your home and it takes two or more days to fill your dishwasher. That's fine. Just think backward. When do you need to make sure you have clean dishes? If you have crazy mornings, then you may need to be sure you are starting your dishwasher just after dinner and emptying it before you go to bed so you can start your day off with an empty dishwasher and clean dishes. You just might have to run your dishwasher when it's not completely full to achieve this. Shocking, I know. It really is okay. Your dishes actually get cleaner when there is space between them anyway. And you can always hand wash the dishes that don't fit in the dishwasher instead of allowing them to stack up. This may be obvious to some folks, but other people struggle with it. Dishwashers make life and homemaking easier, but let's not use them as an excuse for why we don't have enough clean dishes or why dishes are piling up in the sink.

Create a Daily Routine

When I create a routine for my day, I segment the day into five or six chunks of time. Essentially, I'm using an extremely simplified version of a technique commonly referred to as "time blocking." Personally, I think my tweak of this popular method is perfect for busy moms to design an easy-to-follow routine.

I assign large blocks of time for getting things done: morning, mid-morning, afternoon, early evening, and evening. Each block of time represents a portion of the day. Depending on what phase of parenting you're in, your time frames might include: before kids are up, before school, during school, during nap time(s), after school, before dinner, after dinner, and after kids are in bed. Once I segment the day into these blocks of time, I think through what I want to accomplish during each segment. Here's what our daily routine looks like these days:

Morning (before 9:00 a.m.): This is reserved for our morning routines and morning chores.

Mid-morning (9:00 a.m.–noon): Since we homeschool, this is my time to work with my kids (mostly my younger kids at this stage). When my kids were in traditional school, this was when I'd try to get things done around the house, run errands, or take my younger kids to the park.

Afternoon (1:00–5:00 p.m.): My older boys usually have more schoolwork, so they keep working. We sometimes try to do a few small chores during this time, like switching a load of laundry or maybe folding it and putting it away. When we had babies in the house, we had a "nap time" segment in our routine that I used for tackling projects or enjoying a little downtime. I still try to institute a "quiet time" during this time slot, usually from 2:00 to 4:00. I might have the kids play in the backyard, look at books, or play a quiet board game together. This is really my "mom time"—time for me to get a short break.

Early evening (5:00–6:00 p.m.): Typically, I'm prepping dinner if I haven't already thrown something in the crockpot at lunch time. I try to have the kids do a quick cleanup of toys at this time as well.

Evening (6:30 p.m.–bedtime): Evening chores and bedtime routines are done at this time. If everyone finishes early enough, we try to do something fun together before bed. Sometimes we read a chapter in a book together, play card games or board games, watch a TV show, or even rent a movie if it's family fun night.

Your day may be organized differently. As you are filling in your time blocks, ask yourself what your typical day looks like. What is the basic flow of your day? Do you have more time in the morning or in the evenings? If you are like most people, you feel extra ambitious about how much you can get done in the morning. Try to be realistic with how much you schedule into each section of time.

Don't be surprised if you have to move things around a few times to find the right fit for your routine. Piano practice was like that in our home. I first assigned it to the end of our school day, but it was frequently skipped. Either the kids would forget or I would be too tired to remind them. So I moved it to our morning time, and they have become a lot more consistent at practicing.

Devise a Weekly Routine

Once I have our daily routine worked out, I identify what chores need to be done weekly and divide those chores among each family member. For example, everyone in our family does their own laundry on a specific day of the week. This works for us, but it may not for you. You can do your laundry when and how you want—just be sure to add it to your routine. (More laundry tips in chapter 17.)

Monday: Co-op and Crockpot Day. We have our home-school co-op on Mondays. This is essentially a class day where each family in the co-op teaches a class. We love co-op days, but they are long days. I tend to come home and just want to collapse. So on Mondays I plan a crockpot meal. Since it's a busy day, I don't assign any big chores for this day. Our chore is to get out the door on time.

Tuesday: Dust and Vacuum Day. The house gets a quick dust and vacuum on Tuesday mornings as part of our morning chores (done by whoever these chores are assigned to). My younger kids love using disposable dusters. They run around the house dusting all the dusty spots that probably have their names or smiley faces drawn in them. We also do a quick vacuum of our family room, entry way, and kitchen floor with our cordless vacuum. We use a cordless vacuum on our kitchen floor versus sweeping. It's fast and easy. We typically vacuum the kitchen and dining areas every other day (or as needed). However, since the dust bunnies come out of hiding on Tuesdays, vacuuming becomes a must.

Wednesday: Bed Sheets and Bathroom Day (every other week). We strip all the beds in the house and do a mass washing every other Wednesday morning. I have cleaners who come to the house every other Wednesday, so we scurry to get the sheets ready for them to make the beds. (Oh yes, I readily admit to having cleaners. I'll share more on this in chapter 9.) On the opposite Wednesdays, we clean all the bathroom sinks, toilets, and floors.

Thursday: Towels and Trash Day. We used to wash bath and hand towels on each person's personal laundry day, but my younger kids tend to forget. (Gross!) So Thursday is the day we wash all the towels and dishrags, as well as empty all the trash and recycling cans. Since washing towels is the chore assigned to Ashlyn (age eight) right now, she tries to get the load of towels started either before or after she does her own load of laundry. She's become my best laundry helper. My boys all pitch in to take our big trash bins to the curb for Friday pickup. Typically, this job is done in the evening since the bins don't need to be out until the next day.

Friday: Food Day. This is the day I plan the upcoming week's menu and shop for groceries. Since I usually know our weekend plans by Friday, I buy any meal supplies I need for any hosting we may be doing.

TOOLBOX TIP

If a certain day of the week tends to be crazy, don't plan to do much else on that day, and plan ahead for an easy meal.

> ## TOOLBOX TIP
> Make time in your weekly schedule to tackle some of the tasks on your master list.

Weekend: Projects and Parent Laundry Day. With Steve's travel schedule being so varied, I do our laundry on the weekends. This way, if he's traveling the next week, we don't have to scramble to get laundry done before he takes off. On weekends we also try to take on a project or two from our master list. Saturdays are also my errand day. I used to attempt to assign a weekday for errands, but our family schedule is just too busy. So Saturday it is.

YOU'VE GOT THIS!

Learning anything new requires time and repetition. Organization is no different. "Efficiency habits" can be built with some proper planning. The bonus in creating routines for these habits is that you don't have to keep that ongoing list of to-dos in your head. You will already have a game plan for your most common tasks. Figure out the groove that works best for your family—and get dancing.

Unlocking Joy

1. **Figure out your daily and weekly tasks.** You can simply get out a piece of paper or use the "Daily & Weekly Task List" printable found on my site, **KristiClover.com/MOMPrintables**, and keep it on the counter for a week. Write down everything you can possibly think of that needs to get done each day or on specific days.

2. **Time block your routines.** Print a few copies of the "Routine Planner" (also found at the link above) or just write out time blocks for your day. You will be listing EVERYTHING that you do each day and figuring out the best time of day to do it. Use a pencil as you fill in your planner. Remember that you don't need to do all of these tasks. Your kids will also be assigned things to help with. So don't be afraid to start adding family members' initials next to tasks.

Rule #7: Plan Ahead

A Little Bit of Prep Work Goes a Long Way

When my firstborn, Grant, arrived, I did a lot of overplanning. Remember, I was that crazy mom who prepared for a roadside birth. I did things by the book. If it was in print that I needed to have or do something, I took it as gospel. So our first international trip with him—well, it was just Canada, but we did have passports—turned into a circus act. Grant was two months old, and he also had his first cold. Talk about going overboard. This first-time mom not only brought everything you would normally bring for traveling with a newborn but also a pack 'n' play with all the diaper-changing attachments, a baby jungle (you know, those things you put on the floor with toys that dangle), my Baby Björn, an oversized stroller, a breast pump, a bottle sterilizer, and—wait for it—a humidifier. The humidifier was massive and the breast pump was not travel-sized. I had never needed to use the breast pump and Grant had never taken a bottle, but I brought both . . . just in case. I grabbed everything I could think of and everything I'd read about, and took it all with us. It was like I was hoarding on the go. Our luggage cart was almost taller than I was. A forklift would have been more useful, unless the Hulk had been available to help us push the thing. We were quite a sight trying to get from baggage claim to our rental car with our teetering tower of luggage. Needless to say, I had overplanned.

> Overplanning really isn't planning. Proper planning cuts back on excess as much as it prepares for what's coming.

Planning ahead involves more than just packing for a trip or being ready to walk out the door. It takes efficiency into account so that we have what we need—and no more. Planning ahead helps us prepare for the expected things in life, like feeding our family, making purchases that need to be made, planning parties, making holidays fun, and so on. It also helps us be more prepared for the unexpected, like surprise guests, sicknesses, a natural disaster—all of life's little and sometimes big hiccups.

I am well aware that sometimes no amount of planning can stop the "crazy ball" from rolling. Every parent can relate to those moments when you think you are about to get out the door on time and then everything unravels. I've had more days than I care to count when I had everyone in the car only to discover that the baby I was trying to strap into a car seat had a diaper explosion, which required a diaper change—plus a wardrobe change for my child and sometimes for me too. Be it a missing shoe, someone suddenly needing to go to the bathroom, missing car keys—you name it, loading up the car with kids can be challenging.

While we can't control everything, planning ahead can reduce our stress level when chaos begins to creep into our day. For this reason, I'm excited to share some of my best tips for how to plan ahead.

Prepare the Night before to Eliminate Morning Mayhem

If heading out the door for school is part of your normal morning routine, start preparing the night before by making a checklist of all you'll need to do before you leave the house. Your list might include things such as:

> Backpacks ready with completed homework and pencil boxes
> Jackets (I'm told people wear those outside of southern California)
> Shoes and socks by the door
> Lunches packed or planned for (some schools have lunch cards)
> Cell phones charged (for you and any kids who may need a phone)
> Uniforms or clothes for the day clean and ready

If your kids are going on a field trip, make a list of what needs to be packed and ready to go, like permission slips, cash for lunch, or sunscreen. Is there a project that you're going to be tackling the next day or the upcoming weekend? Think through what tools and supplies you'll need. Whatever you have on your list to accomplish soon, make sure you have everything you may need to get that task done.

Regardless of whether I'm planning ahead for something I need to do on a daily, weekly, or monthly basis, I try to figure out what will help me complete all I need to get done as smoothly and efficiently as possible. For instance, I am more likely to take my morning walk when I lay out my workout clothes the night before and put my running shoes next to the door along with my visor. I love listening to podcasts, audiobooks, and music when I'm out on my walks. So I also make sure I have everything downloaded and my headphones placed next to my shoes.

One of the things that took me forever to plan ahead for was my morning devotions. This time is easily hijacked, and I realized I needed a strategy. So I set out everything I wanted to have handy for my devotion time in one spot, such as my Bible, a journal, a few pens, and some index cards (to write down any daily to-dos that pop into my head during this time). My next idea was somewhat brilliant, if I do say so myself. I gathered all my Bible study must-haves and put them in a basket with a handle. This meant that if I had to go to a different room because the kids got up early or were too loud, I could easily make my devotion stash mobile.

Preparing the night before may take several tries to get just right. But it is worth the effort. The day goes so much smoother when I've done a little prep the night before. Setting out the breakfast dishes, laying out clothes for the next day, putting kids' shoes by the door, checking to see if keys are in the right place, making sure the diaper bag is fully stocked, and organizing the day's to-do list are all things you can do the night before to streamline your mornings.

The "Night Before" Planner

Look at your calendar and figure out the best time to start your task. Work backward to set your start time by first figuring out what time you need to leave or have the task done by. If I need to be somewhere at 8:00 a.m., I calculate my drive time and how long it will take me to get ready. Then I set an alarm on my phone for that time to remind myself to start preparing to leave.

Create a checklist for yourself of all the components you will need. What things need to get packed and what things need to get done before you leave? Check them off as you go.

Set out everything you will need to get that task done.
What clothing will you need? If it's a project, what tools
might you need? If lunches need to be packed, set out lunch
boxes already labeled with each child's name and prepack any
food that doesn't need to be refrigerated.

**Put things that will go out the door in one spot or next to
where they will be needed.** Don't have multiple drop spots
for getting ready. Place items right near the door if they are
getting loaded or in one spot for a household task.

Use Checklists to Help You Remember What Needs to Be Accomplished

Several years ago, when I was packing our family once again for a
trip to the snow, I had to rack my brain to remember what I had
packed the year before. It dawned on me that it would be better
to just create a packing list on my computer that I could reference
each time I packed for this type of trip. I took it a step further
and turned the packing list into a checklist. Now all I have to do
if we are going to the snow is to print out the "Snow Trip Packing
List" on my computer and *voila*! We're ready to start packing.

My husband and kids know that if they don't see me writing
something down, then I'll most likely forget it. It's sad but true.
That's why I have lists for just about everything. They help me to
remember what I need to get done, what I need to purchase, and
how to best prepare for what's next on the calendar. I have lists
for babysitters, camping trips, visits with grandparents, car trips,
diaper bag supplies, and beach outings. I even have a "fun list"
with all my ideas for fun meals, activities, outings, and vacations.
After all, fun doesn't always happen spontaneously. Sometimes
we need to plan it into our schedules and prepare a little.

The good news is that because of my lists I don't forget things
as often, and I feel so much more prepared for trips and outings.

To give you a better picture of the types of checklists I use regularly, here are a few examples.

Checklists for our morning routine. I have a big chalkboard in the hallway where I list everything my kids need to do each morning: make the bed, get dressed, eat breakfast, put their dishes in the dishwasher, brush their hair and teeth, and do their morning chores. My older kids rarely have to reference the list, since they've been developing the habit of getting all their morning routines done. My younger kids still need a little help remembering, but I know they will get there too, in time.

Packing checklists for regular outings. We live in a beach town, but I get overwhelmed at the thought of taking our large family to the beach. I finally realized that a list would help me feel less anxious about forgetting something. I'm always looking to simplify how we do things, but if I don't write down what worked well the last time we did something, I forget. So my beach list has had lots of additions to it through the years, like taking gallon jugs filled with water to rinse our sandy feet before we get back into the car. (Steve's brilliant idea.) I also pack baby powder, which is useful for getting dried sand off of arms and legs. I actually laminated this list and have it posted on the inside of a cupboard door near the garage. This way I can reference it easily, and it endures all the little hands that like to pull it down and look at it.

Packing checklists for travel. I have created individual packing lists for each person in the family. They are on my computer and have made getting ready for big trips so much easier. My "readers" pack themselves. My "pre-readers" pack as I read the list to them. All my packing lists for each child are relatively similar but do have some differences. My teens have deodorant and cords for their devices on their packing lists, and my girls have hair bows, brushes, and dresses on theirs. When I had babies and toddlers, my checklist of what I needed to pack for them included essentials for diapering (changing pad, diapers, wipes, rash cream, and resealable plastic bags for stinky diapers), feeding (bibs, bottles, and baby food), and sleeping (pack 'n' play, sheets, blankets, and pacifiers). You get the idea.

What I am about to tell you next just might rock your world. Are you ready? **All my travel packing lists include a meal plan and grocery list!** Let me explain.

One of our favorite places to vacation is Maui. Taking a large family to Hawaii on a budget takes some planning. We try to find places to stay that have a full kitchen and a grill so we don't have to eat out as much. Years ago, I created a set meal plan for when we are on vacation in Hawaii. It's the same meal plan every trip. Our preplanned dinners are simple and easy to throw together. We have spaghetti night, taco night, two barbecue nights with different sides, and one mac and cheese night for the kids (while Steve and I sneak out for a date night). Not only do we save money but I save myself so much time since I don't have to think about what we're going to eat for breakfast, lunch, and dinner or create a grocery list every year. I even have my list broken down by what items to pack and take with us (like spices and my favorite teas), what we'll need to get at Costco (items we can buy in bulk that we'll finish before we go home), and items to get at the local grocery store—all listed out by food type (dairy, fruits, meats, etc.). This helps me to move through the store quickly. I have meal plans for every trip that we go on regularly. The meals are mostly the same but vary a bit depending on where we go. For instance, we don't grill on our snow trips nor eat stew in Hawaii.

Since we fly to Hawaii, I have a special place on my list with notes for everything we need to pack for the kids for the flight, like snacks, gum or lollipops (to keep ears from hurting), coloring books, easy games, headphones for movies or music, and so on. Each of my kids has their own backpack filled and ready to go for the flight. I typically buy a few new books, games, and activities for them, so opening their backpacks on the flight feels a bit like Christmas and keeps them entertained. When we take road trips, I have a similar list of what we'll need for the car ride to keep the kids as happy as they can possibly be while strapped in a seat for hours. (We also bring devices loaded with movies and audio books too, for both types of travel.)

For each of my packing lists for travel, be it for warm weather travel like Hawaii or cold weather travel like snow trips, I have a checklist of things I need to pack for myself and for the room (like card games, resealable plastic bags for snacks, and sleeping bags or pillows), first aid items and medicine (because someone will inevitably get a cough or a stuffy nose while we're gone), and individual packing lists for each child.

Make sure you update your packing checklists as needed. I don't delete my packing lists for babies and toddlers. I just move those items to the last page. Since we've circled back to this life stage several times, I've needed help remembering what to pack for babies when going on various trips. It's also nice to have so you can share it with friends who may be traveling with kids somewhere for the first time (like a snow trip). If, as you are packing, you think of things that aren't on the list, make sure you take a moment to add them to the template on your computer.

· · · · · · · TOOLBOX TIP · · · · · · ·

Pack a freezer meal (or two) to make on the first night of your vacation. I throw everything we need for the recipe into a gallon-sized resealable plastic bag and lay it flat in the freezer. I triple-bag it and slip it into a small insulated travel bag, then pack it just before we hit the road. I've done this for trips we take by car and by plane. (I put a sticky note on the steering wheel so I don't forget to grab it.)

My "Bucket List"

My "bucket list" is quite a bit different than most people's idea of a bucket list. We keep a bucket full of easy-to-use cleaning supplies that my kids can grab and use for most cleaning jobs in the house. So I keep a list of all the cleaning supplies that we'll need for our bucket. As we use up products, we write them down on the whiteboard shopping list hanging in our pantry.

Consolidate Errands: Prepare before You Go!

I try to do all my errands on one day every week. Between the cost of gas and trying not to waste time driving back and forth around town, it helps to be strategic. Trips to a craft store, home decor store, general merchandise store, clothing store, bookstore, warehouse store, hardware store, or even the library all get taken into account on my errand day. On days I go out, **I map out each store or business I need to go to in a driving order that is most efficient.** The key to pulling this all off is making sure that I not only map out my route but that I also have all of my shopping lists, returns, and coupons ready to go and in the car. Often I grab an envelope and put all the receipts and coupons I will need in it. This way things aren't falling out as I go from store to store or getting lost in my purse.

I also keep an ongoing shopping list on my phone for each store I frequent. This way if I am in a store because I need to get a light bulb, I can check the list to see if we need anything else from that store so I don't have to make a second trip.

Sometimes I do my grocery shopping along with my errands, but most times my errands get their very own day. Now, if only I had a full day to leisurely run all my errands . . .

nope. I'm usually doing errands between all the other things we have going on. None of my kids are taking naps anymore, but I remember how difficult it was to run errands when they did. I was trying to race from store to store as fast as possible before my napper would fall asleep in the car and have his or her nap thrown off. I always envied moms whose kids would transfer well from car to crib without waking. My kids typically wouldn't stay asleep if I tried to move them from their car seats.

Plan the Upcoming Week's Menu

Meal planning is near and dear to my heart, since I know it's important to my husband to have a plan for dinner. But I also look at it as a special way that I get to bless my family. Whether you're the one cooking or not, most moms know that the evening rally cry from the children of "What's for dinner?" can be scary when you don't have a plan and are too tired to figure anything out.

Since meal planning falls under the category of kitchen systems, I'm going to wait to lay out my meal planning systems for you in that chapter. Feel free to flip there now if this is a major problem area for you. I just wanted to mention it here, since it is a really important "plan ahead" area for family life.

TOOLBOX TIP

Making shopping lists can help you save money. When you know what you need, it keeps you from guessing and overbuying at the store. I will say that you do have to make sure you stick to your list. If I know we really need an item that's not on the list, then obviously I buy it. But as a general rule, I try to stick to what's on my list.

Have a Backup Plan

Let's face it. Regardless of whether we have kids or not, things don't always go as planned. However, when we have multiple moving parts in our home, we increase the likelihood of having a wrench thrown into our day. So it's crucial to have a backup plan for getting things done—especially for activities that are important.

For example, I try to work out early in the day, but some mornings I don't get out (such as when I have sick kids). My Plan B is to try to exercise during my kids' "quiet time." My Plan C for those days is to pop in an exercise video (you know, the ones collecting dust) or do some stretching or free weights at home. Whether it's exercising, prepping for dinner, doing laundry, running errands, or even just taking your daily shower, figure out other times of the day when you can get those things done. Plan B or C may very well be to skip something for that day (if it's something that can wait) and find another time during the week to get it done.

Plan for interruptions! Having a backup plan helps you better manage your stress level when things start to get a little chaotic. You might even find that your Plan B actually works better for your schedule.

—————————— **YOU'VE GOT THIS!** ——————————

Not everything in life or motherhood can be planned for, but that doesn't mean we shouldn't try to be strategic whenever and wherever we can. Whether it's preparing the night before for the day ahead, making checklists and packing lists, mapping out errands, or creating meal plans, planning ahead is one of the best ways to be better equipped for the unexpected curveballs life throws at us.

Unlocking Joy

1. **What checklists do you want to create for things your family typically does during the week?**

   _____

   _____

   _____

2. **What packing lists could you start typing up to prepare for your next vacation or road trip?**

   _____

   _____

   _____

3. **What activities can you think of to put on your fun list?**

   _____

   _____

   _____

Rule #8: Ask for Help

Bring on the Cavalry

I grew up watching Westerns during the summers I spent with my dad in Oregon as a kid. I think I saw a rerun of every John Wayne movie ever made, whether they were westerns or not. He was the quintessential save-the-day cowboy. Now, you may never have seen or even heard of this popular actor from the 1950s and '60s, but you will probably relate to the all-too-familiar movie moment that has been captured so many times: the hero looks like he or she is beaten and beyond hope, then all of a sudden, help appears from out of nowhere just in the nick of time.

Those are the moments when we catch our breath and release a big sigh of relief. We've all had days when we wished we could look out to the horizon and catch a glimpse of help coming. Reinforcements in our time of need. But most days they don't come right when we need them.

During those exhausting years when I was raising babies and toddlers, I often didn't even have help in the evenings because

Steve was traveling for work. I had no break until the kids were in bed. When we first moved to San Diego, we had no family or friends nearby whom I could call in a pinch. In time we got plugged into a church, and I started meeting other moms—and better still, babysitters. Whenever I picked my kids up from childcare after a moms' event, I'd ask who might be available to babysit.

I tell a story in my book *Sanity Savers for Moms* about how, after the birth of our fourth child, I mustered up the courage to ask for prayer. I may have been asking for prayer, but I was really asking for help. One of the moms in the group had a daughter who was looking for babysitting opportunities and just happened to live three minutes from my house. I learned a big lesson that day: we have to ask for help when we need it.

Asking is the key. Other people couldn't read my mind—and most of the time I probably gave the impression that I had things under control. And I did . . . sometimes. Let's just admit it: asking for help often makes us feel like we are saying we can't manage our homes well on our own. But the reality is that all of us desperately need help during certain seasons and situations.

Now, when it comes to organizing our homes, the same is true. Sometimes we can't do it all on our own and we need to ask for help. There are lots of ways to find help; sometimes we just have to be a little creative.

TOOLBOX TIP

Finding qualified sitters who are safe to leave your kids with can be hard at times. Ask other moms who they use and ask the helpers in Sunday school classes if they are available to babysit. Most churches run basic background checks on their childcare assistants, so that may be a good option. Families with teenagers may also be a resource for you to enlist some help.

Accept Help When Offered

There are times when we see the help coming over the horizon but for some reason we turn it away. I know I've turned people away when they offered to help out because I didn't know what to have them help with. "Want to come over and help me fold laundry?" just seemed like an awkward thing to ask someone to do.

While I haven't always said yes to offers of help, I have always been grateful those times that I did. When our friends (the family of six) who were living with us moved out, a girlfriend offered to help me put my house back together. I needed to reorganize rooms and switch up who slept where. Normally, I wouldn't worry about having extra things in the hallways while I was trying to organize. However, a well-known company was coming over to interview me about "home organization during the holidays," which meant I had a deadline. I had to get my whole house not only put together but also decorated for Christmas. Sometimes there are not enough hours in the day to get things done. So when my sweet friend said she could help, I readily accepted her offer. If I had to take a few moments to figure out how I wanted things done, my friend just hung out with the kids or helped them clean up a game they'd been playing. Project after project, she hung in there and just kept asking what was next. What would have taken me days ended up only taking hours.

Since I speak about accepting help from others when offered, I think it is easier for me to say yes. (How can I say no when I tell other moms to say yes?) I wish that just reading these words would make you feel that same obligation to say yes when others volunteer to lend a hand. I know it's humbling to invite others over to witness your mess. Just remember, no one expects you to be perfect.

Hire Some Help

Yep, I hire a couple to come to my house every other week to do a basic cleaning: change the sheets, clean the bathrooms and kitchen, dust, vacuum, and mop. I'm so grateful every time they're here. I hug them as they leave and thank them profusely throughout their time in my home.

Just because I hire some help doesn't mean I don't have to do any cleaning. For one thing, I have to do some tidying before the cleaners arrive so they can get to what they need to clean. It seems a bit counterintuitive to "clean" before the cleaners come, but we do. Beyond that, with seven "moving parts" in our house, there is cleaning to be done each and every day.

If you don't have money in your budget for cleaners to come to your house regularly, you might consider hiring help for a special project or for a season. Maybe all you need is someone to come once or twice a year to do a deep clean.

Just after our fifth child was born, I needed some extra help getting the house ready for two groups we were going to be hosting on a weekly basis. I thought through what I needed clean before these two groups came over (one on Wednesday nights and the other on Thursday mornings) and also determined how much money I could spend on the extra housecleaning. My cleaners were able to stay within the budget and do all the things I needed done. So for a season they came to our home every week, alternating between our normal biweekly clean and just the kitchen and the downstairs bathrooms and floors.

Enlist a Decluttering Buddy

When it's time to declutter, consider asking a friend to help. Not only does the job go faster but your friend isn't as emotionally attached to your stuff as you are. She can help you sort through and get rid of things you may be tempted to keep.

Spouses can be great for this role too. My husband will look at a massive pile of "love notes" from our kids and know that we don't need to keep every single one. I, on the other hand, look at each and flash back to when my kids were littler and made each masterpiece for me as an expression of their love. Don't be afraid to speak up for things that are special, but be reasonable. I didn't need forty love notes—a few were enough to capture the memories.

Another great way to use a buddy system is to swap childcare. If you are struggling with having someone see your mess at the peak of its glory, ask a friend to watch your kids at her house for a few hours while you work hard to make a dent in your project. Then trade off another day so that she can get a break to do whatever she needs to do. Believe it or not, I'm doing just that today as I write this chapter. (See, I do take my own advice.)

Train Your Kids to Help

> We all need help when it comes to figuring out how to get our mess makers to pitch in and demess the house.

If *decluttering* is a word, then *demessing* should be one too. That's exactly what our house needs daily—demessing!

I believe it's important to train all my kids to work in our home. My kids aren't going to live in our house forever and they'll need to know how to cook, clean, and do the dishes and laundry once in a while. There's no way to foresee how life is going to play out. Our kids may marry someone who has no clue how to manage a home or they may not get married at all. Only God knows the details of their futures. And if and when they do get married, I want them to be able to contribute to the care and maintenance of their homes. My parenting goals include training my kids to not only have exceptional character but also to be thoughtful, loving spouses and parents.

Every person in my house contributes to the state of order in our home. I think it is important to not only train my kids to help with basic housework but also to learn the ins and outs of managing a home. Besides, the more your kids learn now about how to keep their rooms and the rest of the house clean and organized, the easier it will be for them to maintain order in their own homes someday. You're a team! Each person should be pitching in. So enlist your teammates to help you. Here are some ideas for how to do just that.

Start them young. Young kids can do a lot more than some might think. While two-year-olds can't carry out heavy trash bags, they can put kitchen utensils away, pick up toys, and put their shoes in a basket. Three- and four-year-olds can be taught to wipe down the kitchen table, dust with a disposable duster, and put away some laundry with a little direction.

Young kids can see housework as fun if you present it as such. All of my kids loved helping around the house when they were little. The younger they are trained, the more efficient they become as they get older.

Don't expect perfection. It will take a lot of time and practice in order for your kids to learn to do jobs around the house to your satisfaction, so you may need to lower your standards. For example, one of my girls' favorite jobs when they were ages six and four was folding the dish towels and hand towels. I'd dump the load on the floor and they would go to town folding. They didn't always get the corners matched perfectly, but I didn't care. These towels got tucked away in a drawer, so it didn't really matter. Plus, my girls were proud of their hard work—and I never want to do or say anything to take away from that.

TOOLBOX TIP

It's often hard to think through what chores to give to kids at various ages. I'm always asking friends what they have their kids doing around the house to help out. I love getting ideas about what other chores I should be training my kids to do.

Praise them for their work. It's important to praise your kids for their effort, so fight the urge to overcorrect. Training is great, but it has to be done with gentleness and positivity. Instead of refolding a towel that was folded rather hastily, I just grab another towel and join my child in the folding. Sometimes I even talk through what I'm doing as I fold so they can see how to do the work. Kids learn when they work side by side with you.

> Help your kids feel like they are a valuable part of your family team.

Think of them as little interns. As I just mentioned, when it comes to housework, kids learn best by your side. Make it fun and think of it as more time to spend together. If you were training an intern for a job, you would walk them through lots of steps and show them over and over again how the job is supposed to be done. So be patient and keep lovingly training your kids how to do different tasks and projects. Yes, it's faster to just do it yourself, but it will be worth the time and energy in the long run.

TOOLBOX TIP

One great way for training kids how to do a job is to take a picture of the completed job. If you want the counter near the sink to be dish-free at the end of the night, take a picture of everything clean and put away and show it to your kids so they know what the counter should look like when they are done. If you are working on folding skills, take a picture of how you want various things folded so your kids can use it for reference. You can laminate the photos and even use them as part of your chore system or just post them near where the work will be done.

Involve them in planning. Before I put together our household routines at the start of a new school year, I grab a large whiteboard and together with my kids list all the things we have going on and the work that needs to be done regularly. When they are part of the planning process, they can see the importance of finishing tasks at the predetermined time of day in our routine instead of simply putting things off for later. "Later" they may have something else going on or other chores to do. It also teaches them the importance of creating a routine and figuring out the best way to accomplish work. More life training!

Train your way out of a job. Please don't laugh, but I teach my kids to do my least-favorite jobs first. Laundry, dishes, and trash are all on that list. I don't say anything negative about the job; I just train them and encourage them as they learn it.

———— YOU'VE GOT THIS! ————

I hope this chapter has helped you understand that it's okay not to be able to do everything on your own. It's vital to your sanity to ask for and accept help—and to train your live-in helpers. So before you raise the white flag in surrender to the mess, look for creative ways to get help—and bring on the cavalry!

Unlocking Joy

1. **What holds you back from asking others for help?** If you struggle with asking for help, try to figure out why you hesitate to reach out.

_____

_____

_____

2. **Make a list of potential helpers.** Now is a great time to create a list of possible babysitters and friends you'd feel comfortable trading childcare with so that you can get time alone in your house to work on projects—or time alone for rest.

_____

_____

_____

3. **What are some chores you can think of right now that your kids could learn to do in addition to what they are already doing?**

_____

_____

_____

10

Rule #9: Don't Eat
of the Bread of Idleness

Overcoming Laziness and Avoidance

My friends laugh at me when I tell them I struggle with laziness and misusing my time. I have five kids, homeschool, write books, and run a small business from my home, so how would I ever *have time* to waste? Yet I do. It's all too easy for me to have the kids go outside to play or watch a show upstairs after we're done with school. Then I can plop myself down in front of the TV and watch a couple of Hallmark movies. Throw in a sweet or salty snack, and I've got myself a lazy afternoon.

When I was growing up, the television was on—a lot. I turned it on when I got home from school, and during the summer I watched it throughout the day. It didn't matter if I'd seen a movie multiple times. I'd watch it again. Watching TV and turning off my brain became a habit. A bad habit that can keep me from being productive. Not that it's wrong to watch an occasional movie or TV show, but I can take it to the extreme if I'm not careful. Now, in this season of my life, I watch a lot less TV than I used to—and I sometimes joke about the fact that this is how I've been able to find time to write and get so many things done.

Don't get me wrong. Some seasons of motherhood require a lot from us physically, making it vital for moms to have downtime and rest. So I encourage moms to create time in their schedules to get a little quiet and to do things they enjoy. However, there is a difference between taking some time to get a little R & R and squandering time. Everyone has their own areas of weakness; mine just happens to be watching too much TV—and, well, maybe Instagram.

> The beauty is that when we learn more efficient ways to tackle the issues in our home, we actually free up our time to do more of the things we love. But first we have to overcome inertia and just get started.

The Problem with Procrastination

When I really don't want to do something, I can fill my time with any and every other thing I can in order to postpone the inevitable, unavoidable work that needs to get done—like housework. Nobody wakes up and feels excited that today is the day they get to mop floors or clean toilets. But those chores have to get done eventually. Otherwise all that undone work starts to add up—as does the stress. As the mess accumulates, it becomes harder and harder to muster the energy or willpower to get started. Too much procrastination only leads to more frustration.

> The longer we remain idle, the more craziness will ensue—and our inner organizer will just want to keep napping.

This is why I recommend doing your "worst thing" first. You'd be surprised just how much better you'll feel once you have tackled the thing that drives you crazy. That forward momentum is sometimes just the motivation we need to get going on other tasks.

I thought I'd share where the title for this chapter, "Don't Eat of the Bread of Idleness," came from. You may have been wondering if I found it in a fortune cookie. Well, early in my marriage, even before kids, I came upon a Bible verse that really stood out to me . . . probably because I was struggling with mismanaging my time (aka procrastination). It was Proverbs 31:27, "She watches over the affairs of her household and does not eat the bread of idleness." Anytime I notice that I'm not really using my time wisely, this verse comes to mind because I don't want idleness to define me or impact my household negatively. I actually wrote this verse out and taped it above my TV for a season.

It is really important for us to find ways to motivate ourselves to stop procrastinating and stop avoiding work around the house that needs to get done. One of the ways many of us procrastinate when it comes to dealing with our mess is to simply hide it away.

Hiding the Mess = Avoidance

The fact that I love organizing and have been speaking on it for so long only makes it that much more embarrassing when friends come over and I haven't cleaned up. Oh, the pressure! Yet I want to be real too. I can stuff things in a closet and pretend I have it all together (as the story about my little red wagon illustrates) or I can say, "Come on in! Welcome to our mess. We haven't had a chance to clean up, but I'm so happy you are here."

Most people hide clutter instead of dealing with it. We've all seen those shows or movies where the character sweeps crumbs under a rug. That's essentially what we're doing when we "sweep" our mess into a closet or bin. It just seems easier to move the mess

117

than to take the time to go through it and put things away where they belong. But while it may not be visible, it's still there. You'd be surprised by how many homes have a garage, closets, cupboards, and drawers filled with clutter that has been tucked away neatly out of sight. When this is our tendency, storage systems can be dangerous. Those pretty baskets and extra plastic bins begin to store our to-do piles instead of the things we actually need.

> Just tucking things out of the way is not organizing. We need to take the time to put things where they truly belong.

A few years ago, a girlfriend asked me to help her organize her kitchen. At first glance, it looked neat and organized. Not much was on the counters and she had bins in her cupboards to sort things. It wasn't until I started looking in those cupboard bins that I realized what was going on. There were no designated spaces for anything! The cupboards and drawers had become a free-for-all. I found tea bags in three different bins, nuts in two, and cereal boxes on several different shelves. To combat this kind of organizational challenge, I recommend that people assign a designated space for things and then label that space so everyone knows what belongs there. Putting things in their designated space makes it less likely that you will end up with duplicates or similar items in multiple places.

So, in order to help my friend create better storage locations for the items in her kitchen, I asked her some of my *functional organization* questions (we'll get to what these are in chapter 13). We organized items according to their use and decided what would go in each bin and on each shelf. I even helped her figure out a way to move her pantry items to her kitchen space so she didn't have to walk around the corner to the hall closet where they'd been stored. She loved it.

Hiding clutter is a horrible habit. It only complicates the problem. So do yourself a favor and don't put it off any longer: start organizing, bit by bit.

Making Time to Get Things Done

We all have the same twenty-four hours in our day. Some days seem to go soooo slowly and others seem to zip by. Somehow, regardless of what fills our days, we have to make time to get organized and to stay organized. There's no getting around it, unless you want to end up on an episode of one of those hoarding shows.

How do we find time to address the needs of our home? Well, we make time. Schedules may have to be cleared and rearranged a bit to create pockets of time to do what needs to be done. Hopefully, you'll find some of these "time-making" techniques that I've used through the years helpful.

> **Eliminate time-wasters from your day and your schedule.** Be honest with yourself as you examine your calendar.

> **Look for ways you can more wisely use your time.** Maybe there are ways you can group tasks together to work more efficiently if they are similar or in the same room.

> **Focus your attention on just one task at a time.** Some tasks require focused attention. Trying to multitask is not always the answer. You may need to work on just one thing at a time.

> **Make sure your weekly routine includes time to organize.** Eventually, your organization routine will become a new habit.

> **Put your phone away and silence app notifications so you don't get distracted.** Putting your phone in another

room and turning off app notifications helps keep you focused, since your phone won't be buzzing as often.

> **Consider a digital and electronic fast.** Yikes! I know that sounds extreme, but you'd be surprised how much time you get back just by staying off all your electronic devices (or maybe just social media). I'm not asking you to go a month, but consider several hours or even a few days.

> **Play a "beat the clock" game.** Use a timer to give yourself a set time to start and stop. Some families use this technique to get evening chores done. Everyone runs around as fast as they can, picking up and getting things done before the timer chimes.

> **Use a timer to remind yourself to do things.** If I have to be out the door at a certain time, I set my timer for twenty minutes before I need to leave to give myself time to stop what I'm doing and get ready. Timers are great for reminding yourself to switch loads of laundry too.

> **Make your homemaking and organizing a priority.** In reality, getting organized helps you to create more time to get to all the other priorities in your life.

I get it. Finding time to declutter and organize your home can be difficult. But even when life is busy, it's important to get some work done. Stick to the necessities if you need to, but don't throw in the towel completely. If you need extra hands to get things done around the house, then ask those living under your roof to pitch in where you need them to, or ask a friend. Again, you should never hesitate to ask for help when you need it.

Use Rewards and Make It Fun

Sometimes I motivate myself to work by rewarding myself once the task is accomplished. For instance, I might tell myself that when I am done washing, folding, and putting away the laundry, I can sit down and look at my Instagram feed for a bit. Or I'll tell the kids that if we clean out the garage and take a few loads to the Salvation Army, then we'll order pizza and make root beer floats for dinner that night.

Since hospitality is near and dear to my heart, I often think of food rewards. Lemonade for a hot day's work outside. Cookies or hot chocolate at the end of a cold, wintry day of decluttering. My kids know that when we have guests over, we typically have some sort of delicious dessert that they'll get to enjoy, which creates a little extra incentive for them to pitch in and help us get ready for company.

Rewards don't have to be lavish. And they don't have to be food-related either. Active rewards work great too. Family hikes, a beach day, or even a pedicure with a friend are all things that have helped me focus on getting the work done and staying on top of the mess.

Sometimes just completing a project is all the motivation I need. "Done" feels good. For me, getting to put a big, fat checkmark on my to-do list often feels like a reward. However, I know I'm a bit obsessive when it comes to my lists. I'm the person who will add something to my list just so I can check it off. You need to figure out what motivates you best. Consider creating a list of things that you think would be fun rewards for getting some big projects off your plate. Maybe you want to buy a much-needed piece of furniture for a room. Make that purchase your reward for cleaning out all your kitchen cupboards and putting everything in a designated spot.

When we find ways to make our work more enjoyable, we're more likely to jump in and get started. I love listening to music, podcasts, or audiobooks when I'm doing work around the house that doesn't require a lot of concentration. The work seems to go faster when I'm distracted. So when I'm folding clothes, tidying up a room, or even decluttering an area, I will listen to something

I enjoy either through my headphones or a portable speaker. I've also been known to put on a movie while sorting through bins or doing some other project. I don't feel lazy when I'm being productive while watching something.

Changing Your Mindset and Adjusting Your Attitude

Believe it or not, at times I have a stinky attitude about caring for our home, especially when our schedule is too busy and the house is driving me crazy. Home management is a never-ending job. Whether you stay on top of the mess or not, the work is always there. And even though I am passionate about organizing and have experienced its benefits, the thoughts in my brain at the end of a long day don't always agree with that sentiment. There are times when I feel unappreciated and undervalued by my family, and these types of thoughts fill my brain: *No one thanked me for picking up their mess or tidying that room. Do they even realize that I do more work than everyone combined in this house? Do they notice that I clean up their messes more than they do? Do they just think I'm their servant?*

Obviously there are times when a family meeting is in order and conversations need to happen. Maybe even a little training in gratitude and diligence. But more often than not, it comes down to my attitude. What I've realized is that I have a choice about whether or not to focus my thoughts on the negative. Yes, it takes a lot of work to have a well-organized home. Yes, I might be doing the bulk of the work right now. Yes, no one may have thanked me today or even this week. However, I have to make a choice as to whether to let these types of thoughts affect my attitude and my joy.

Attitude is a choice. Sometimes I just have to rise above those negative thoughts and choose to be a fun-loving, joy-filled mom and wife who is blessed to have a home to manage. Instead of focusing on the negative, I try to focus on the flip side:

> ❯ Those shoes and socks are not in their baskets again, *but* I'm blessed to have little feet in my home that wear those shoes and socks.
>
> ❯ Steve is traveling yet again, and I am exhausted by the extra work that creates for me, *but* I'm blessed that he has a job that keeps a roof over our heads and food on the table.
>
> ❯ There is always a lot of stuff to manage and things to get done around my home, *but* I'm blessed to have my family, my home, and a body capable of getting the work done.

This kind of "big picture" thinking snaps me out of my stuck-in-the-mud thoughts, and suddenly housekeeping doesn't seem so bad. Changing my mindset and focusing on what I'm grateful for has helped me to be more positive and joyful about the things that I have to get done.

YOU'VE GOT THIS!

Mess happens. Laziness happens. Exhaustion happens. In the hustle and bustle of life, it's easy to put off all the little and big jobs we need to get done around the house. When we learn to use our time better and change our mindsets, it becomes easier to view work as a blessing. Just remember to give yourself lots of grace when it comes to organizing, especially if you are in a season of your life when things are crazy.

Unlocking Joy

1. **What are you doing too much of that is possibly a misuse of your time?** Too much screen time, whether email, social media, videos, or TV, tends to be a big time-sucker in this day

and age. You might consider tracking your day to see what you're spending your time doing.

_____

_____

_____

2. What are some ways you can create time to get organized?

_____

_____

_____

3. What rewards can you use to motivate yourself or your family to tackle some of the big projects on your to-do list?

_____

_____

_____

11

Rule #10: Stick with It!

Getting Organization to Stick

Stickiness is not always a good thing in a houseful of kids. It can be downright scary at times. There are days I feel something sticky and I really don't want to know what it is. I just want it off. However, when it comes to getting and staying organized, a heavy dose of "stickiness" is required: stick-to-it-ness!

Organization is not something we do only once and never have to do again, unfortunately. We have to stay at it, keep going, and not give up. Whether we call it endurance, tenacity, determination, or stick-to-it-ness, we need it to keep ourselves from falling right back into the same old habits. There is an element of diligence that needs to be applied in order to have lasting results. I've found that when I persevere with staying organized, I find joy rather than drudgery in the management of my home. I believe you will too.

> Knowing how to get organized is only half the battle. Actually doing the hard work of getting organized—and then staying on top of the mayhem—is the other half of the fight.

Make Staying Organized a Habit

There is a lot of information on the internet offering tips and techniques for how to get organized. Most of these techniques will help us achieve some level of order. And applying the nine "rules" we've already covered will definitely help us to get organized. However, the bigger challenge is how to *stay* organized and maintain the order we've worked so hard to achieve. Home organization is a lot like dieting. Lots of plans will work to get us organized (or get the weight off), but the maintenance part of dieting—and organization—is often where things fall apart. It's hard to make staying organized a habit, and many people downright fail at this.

Learning how to make staying organized a regular part of our homemaking "diet" (or daily routine) is vital to keeping our home "in shape." So how can we get all our organizing to "stick"? This chapter is designed to help you identify a few of the most common failing points and understand how mayhem sneaks back into your home, as well as tips on how to make order stick around.

Little Messes Add Up Fast!

Have you ever cleaned up a room, then looked around and thought, *Wow! I love the way this room feels when it's clean. I'm never going to let it get messy again!*? I always think that "this time" it will be different or easier since I did all the hard work of cleaning up and decluttering. But then we let one little mess slide.

Then another. And another. Suddenly we're right back where we started. Maybe not with quite as much clutter hiding away as before, but the chaos has taken over yet again.

In a perfect world, you and every other person in your home would tidy up after themselves throughout the day. Some people are wired like this. Even some kids are wired like this. But most aren't. I have taught each of my kids to put away anything they get out before they move on to the next toy or game or leave the room, but that doesn't mean they always do it. If I'm not in the room to make sure they follow through, the place may end up looking like a bomb went off. I like to think of it as a creativity explosion. All that to say, mess happens throughout the day. Dishes pile up. Toys are strung across the room. Clothes are on the floors in bedrooms. Regardless of whether I've told myself after a major cleanup that we'll keep the house looking great and organized forever, the reality is that things start creeping onto the counters and floors eventually. The busier our schedules are, the more easily things accumulate.

This is why it's crucial to get ahead of the big messes by tackling the little messes as they pop up—even when you feel exhausted.

When You Just Don't Have the Energy

When the kids are all tucked in bed and I come downstairs and find things left undone, the last thing I want to do is clean another dish. I know I'm not the only person to feel like this. We often feel tapped out and just don't have the energy to pick one more thing up. Although we want our homes to be clean, tidy, and ready for company, we lack the stick-to-it-ness due to exhaustion—and sometimes we just can't be bothered to do anything about the mess we see around us.

But you know what? I've found that the more I streamline my home management, the more time I actually get to rest and do fun things. This is why I've spent so much time figuring out the most efficient ways to get organized in my home, schedule, and life. I was looking for freedom. **I didn't want the state of my house to dominate my life.** That alone became a major motivator for me. Now as I walk through the house picking up any remaining clutter before sitting down at night, this mantra runs through my head: *Diligence first, then rest.*

Of course, there is one way to try to circumvent these "too tired to clean up" moments . . . and that's figuring out a time earlier in the day to do it, when you have more energy and your helpers are around to pitch in.

Have a Set Time of Day to Tidy Up

It takes less energy in the long run to take a few moments each day to tidy up than to put off trying to repair the damage of house disarray until the end of a busy day, week, or month. If you haven't already, it's a good idea to add an evening cleanup to your routine. My family's set time for this is either right after dinner every day or around 7:00 p.m. During this "tidy time," each person in the family goes around the house picking up toys, making sure the kitchen counters are clear of dishes and papers, and completing any chores.

Here's an overview of what we do to tidy up each day:

Family room: Put away any blankets or pillows that have been used throughout the day for lounging on the floor or creating forts. Fluff the cushions on the couch and put the decorative pillows back in place. Pick up and put away all toys, art projects, coloring pages, Nerf bullets, and games.

Kitchen: Load the dishes into the dishwasher and hand wash any that remain. Dry and put away all clean dishes. Wipe down the counters and the cutting board. Make sure the

TOOLBOX TIP

Be sure your family's "tidy time" isn't too close to bedtime. Kids tend to lollygag if they think they can prolong bedtime and stay up later.

table is clear of stuff and wipe it down if needed. Vacuum the floor if it needs de-crumbing.

Hallways: Pick up and put away any shoes or clothes that are out or lying around. Schoolwork that was brought downstairs gets filed or put back on an individual's desk upstairs.

Bedrooms: Everyone is supposed to make sure their clothes from the day actually made it into the hamper and that toys are picked up in their own rooms. Note my choice of words. They are "supposed" to get this done, but it's not unusual to find this evening chore left undone. (If it's too late in the evening, they are required to do it in the morning.)

Once again, what works for our family may not work for yours. I have some friends who tidy up three or more times a day, typically after breakfast, after lunch, after dinner, and before bed. This works great in some homes and situations, but not all. If you find that you just can't handle saving all the cleaning up for the end of the day and would rather just collapse on the couch, then figure out a different time of the day when you're not as worn out.

The more you make tidying up a habitual part of your daily routine, and get everyone in the house to help, the easier it will be to stay on top of the chaos. There are always going to be nights here and there when things get missed by the kids. Those are the nights I dig deep and just get it done. Nike was onto something with their motto: "Just do it."

Create "Rules" for Problem Areas

Whenever I notice the same area is being left messy day after day, I create some rules for myself or for my household. For example, when I noticed that the room we keep our electronic piano in continually had headphones left out, music sheets scattered about, and the bench pulled out, I created a few "piano room" rules: turn off the piano when done, hang up the headphones, tuck the bench neatly under the piano, and put away music books or sheets neatly in the basket next to the piano. Our piano room is also our living room and is located near the front door. I always try to keep the front areas of our home picked up so we are ready for unexpected company. Even if the back of the house is a little crazy, at least this section is straightened and welcoming. My piano room rules help me to achieve this goal.

Another rule is that my kids have to get out a blanket before playing with small toys, beads, or LEGOs. This rule helps to keep these "painful when stepped on" toys in one contained area (and not hidden in the carpet).

Having set rules for how a room should be kept clean helps the whole family to know what the expectations are for that area.

Put the Right System in Place

More often than not, it doesn't take as long as I thought it would to clean up a space—*especially* when I'm using good systems. If you are feeling like you're spinning your wheels or picking up the same mess every day, it may be that you don't have the right system in place for that area or those items. **A system is really nothing more than an organized way to get something done. Systems help you to streamline tasks that you do regularly.** In phase II we're going to dive much deeper into some of the systems I use to stay organized, but I want to give you an example of how having a good system in place can even help your kids remain organized.

My kids used to leave shoes, socks, and sweatshirts on the floor everywhere. Drove me crazy. One child did this as he was walking. One shoe to the left and one shoe to the right. Here a sock. There a sock. Everywhere a sock-sock. It was almost comical, but not day after day. I realized I didn't have an easy, workable system for my kids to put their clothes and shoes away, and I was allowing them to develop some bad habits. So I bought stackable drawers for all the shoes of the house and tucked it in a closet. Each child is responsible for taking off their shoes when they come in the door and putting them away in their own drawer—and their dirty socks are supposed to be taken to the hampers in their rooms. (It's not fun finding a stockpile of dirty socks in the shoe drawers.) The hook solution I told you about earlier addressed the sweatshirt problem. It still surprises me that all I had to do to help my kids get into the habit of keeping these items picked up was to buy a few stackable drawers and some stick-on hooks—and then, of course, to train them to use them!

Identifying where messes continue to collect and coming up with solutions to the problem are what creating systems is all about. Just take on one problem area at a time, and soon you'll discover that staying on top of clutter is a lot easier.

TOOLBOX TIP

When teaching kids to learn new habits, I've found it helps to offer them a reward for learning that habit. I've used sticker charts and jars to keep track of the times a child follows through on a habit I am trying to teach him or her. Once the chart or jar is filled from their "acts of diligence," then I take the child out for frozen yogurt.

Periodic Decluttering

Ideally, we'd never have to repeat the decluttering process since we'd become so mindful of what we allow to collect in our home. However, realistically, it's a good idea to do periodic decluttering of storage areas and other clutter-collecting places in our homes. Depending on how well we've stayed on top of things, this could be an easy job or it could feel like we're starting from scratch again. Either way, we all should be sure to plan to do at least one focused declutter of our home each year. I usually choose the summer to do a little "spring cleaning" and decluttering. We typically have less going on at that time, and I can get my whole family involved.

Accountability Makes a Huge Difference!

If you think you might need some help sticking with it, consider asking a friend or two to hold you accountable for getting and staying organized. Ask them to check in on you from time to time to see how things are going—or, better yet, to come and see your finished work. It feels so good to share your success and hard work with a friend.

Most things are more enjoyable with friends. Knowing this, I created a fun way to put this book into action: Host a "M.O.M.s Night In." We're all familiar with the concept of a "moms' night out," but I'm going to change it up a bit: pick a home to meet together with friends and spend an evening encouraging one another on how to implement the strategies in this book.

If you go to **KristiClover.com/MOMsNightIn**, you can sign up to receive a special "M.O.M.s Night In" video from me along with all the printables to use that night with your friends. I guess you can say this is my way of trying to be there and enjoy your night of fellowship with you. Oh, how I wish I could just show up and hang out for the evening! That would be amazing. In lieu of me physically being there to encourage you, I can at least make a digital appearance. The evening is meant to be light-hearted and fun. These special "M.O.M.s Night In" printouts are different from the ones that go along with the book (the ones at KristiClover.com/MOMPrintables). They are streamlined and meant to be filled out in a group setting. I've even included a few delicious recipes that you can all enjoy together. (Yes, now you are really wishing I could just show up . . . with food in hand!)

So head over and sign up to get all the details. I've done most of the planning for you. This is hospitality made easy.

Not ready to host anything? No problem. You can do this with friends or family who are out of the area too. You can still hold each other accountable by going through the book and printables at the same time and taking some before-and-after photos to share with each other. Just have some fun with it.

YOU'VE GOT THIS!

I want you to finish strong. I don't want this to be a book that collects dust that you'll never get around to dusting. You can step out of the mess and experience freedom from the chaos and mayhem that motherhood can often bring with it.

When it comes to getting sticky with your home organization, think about this. If you pick just one thing to work on, just one area, project, or routine, and stick with it—you are doing great! Getting organized doesn't mean that your house has to be ready for a *Better Homes & Gardens* photo shoot. It means that you are creating efficiency in your home so that your family can thrive. Remember: progress, not perfection.

Look at your crazy to-do list and just pick one thing to start tackling. Break it down and attack. You can do it! Don't give up! Get sticky!

Unlocking Joy

1. **When is the best time(s) of day for you to create your own family "tidy time"?**

   _____

   _____

   _____

2. **What area of your home tends to be the hardest to maintain order in?** Can you think of any strategies or rules that might help this area to be easier to keep tidy?

   _____

   _____

   _____

3. **Can you think of any friends who might enjoy doing a "M.O.M.s Night In" with you?** Write their name below and contact them to see if they'd be interested in joining you, then get a date on the calendar. (Be sure to head over to **KristiClover.com/MOMsNightIn** to get all the details you'll need to plan your night of fun!)

   _____

   _____

   _____

THE
FRAMEWORK

The Systems That Will Make
Your Home More Efficient

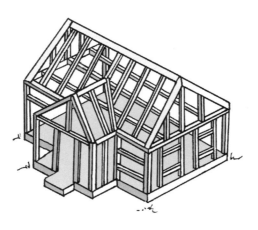

Decluttering Systems

Easy Steps for Crushing the Clutter

We've already talked about decluttering, but in this chapter we're going to deconstruct exactly how to do it—because we can't get organized until we've dealt with all the clutter. I'm not saying we need to become minimalists, even though having less stuff to keep organized does make it easier to stay on top of our homes. We do, however, have to get serious about the excess we tend to keep around.

Clutter accumulates quickly, so there is no better time than *now* to start ridding your home of it. I suggest that you pick a day and time to work on a decluttering project and then go for it. I enjoy decluttering, mostly because it feels so good when I'm done. Maybe it also has a bit to do with the fact that I reward myself after big projects are completed. I throw myself a little decluttering after-party. The kids will celebrate anything with me if it involves pizza or ice cream, though I'll admit that after big decluttering projects I'd prefer a spa day.

Here's how to get started.

Pick a Room to Declutter

There are a lot of different ideas about the best place to start decluttering your home. Here are a few suggestions. Choose the one that works best for you.

> Start in a room you use a lot and want cleaned up.
> Start in a room that is easy to declutter so you have one room you can quickly check off your list.
> Start in a room from your master list that has lots of A priorities—those tasks that you've decided should "absolutely" get done sooner rather than later.
> Start in the garage so you have a clean space to store things that need to come out of your house. This may even help you kill two birds with one stone if your garage is on your "worst thing" list: your worst thing *plus* decluttering!
> Start with categories. This technique was made popular by Marie Kondo, a Japanese superstar decluttering expert, and is referred to as the "KonMari" method. She organizes by categories versus a more traditional room-by-room approach. She suggests starting with clothes, then books, then papers, then miscellaneous items, and then finally anything with sentimental value.*

As I'm sure you've picked up on, I prefer to declutter room by room. I like the feeling of having a completely clean and organized space. It motivates me to keep going in the rest of the house. When I'm doing a big purge, I start in the garage. This is usually where I find most of my clutter. Things I wanted out of sight before guests came over, toys and clothing my kids have outgrown, potential garage sale items—all tend to end up in our

*Marie Kondo, *The Life-Changing Magic of Tidying Up: The Japanese Art of Decluttering and Organizing* (Ten Speed Press, 2014), 119.

garage. The problem is, things that are "out of sight" also stay "out of mind." I used to justify keeping clutter in the garage by telling myself that if it's not in the house and I'm not tripping on it, then I can keep it. Not the best approach. I also start in the garage in order to create space for things that truly deserve a place in it.

You, however, can start wherever your heart desires—just start! (I will say that if you have a main living area that is in desperate need of some decluttering—and your sanity is being threatened—it might be best to start there.) As you conquer a room or space, check it off your master list and celebrate.

Note: if you can't find time to declutter an entire room, you can still "spot declutter." Much like you might spot clean a stain, you can tackle one part of a room at a time. Maybe it's a bookshelf, a drawer, a closet, the space under a bed, or your pantry. As much as it would be great if you could take a week off to declutter your entire house, this might not be reasonable. Just clean what you can. That's what's important.

Get a Vision for the Space

Once you have chosen which room to declutter, step back and take a breath. Don't get stressed out. Just relax. Remember, it's going to feel so good when you are done. Then think through what you want that space to be used for.

Maybe a bedroom that was being used as office space is no longer needed for that function, and a new craft room is in order. Maybe your kids have outgrown their room's current decor. I know my teens didn't want the cute train and car decor or the sports-themed vinyl wallpaper stickers to remain on their walls. So we change things up in their rooms from time to time. I turned our mostly unused living room into a study and music room by moving some bookshelves together to form a wall of books (I swoon just thinking about that room). I love books, and having all my favorites in one place makes me happy. By adding a big, oversized chair to one corner of the room, I created a cozy reading nook. Between the couch we already had in the room and my new chair, we now have enough seating for our whole family to sit together for our own family-style piano recitals.

Having a vision for the space will help you to determine what really needs to stay in that room. Think through what activities you would like to have happen in each space. If something doesn't bring value to the function of the room (or space), then it probably doesn't belong there.

Empty the Whole Area

Now, I don't expect you to hire movers when you declutter. However, there are spaces, such as the garage, closets, and bookcases, that are best to declutter by taking everything out first. While you don't need to move furniture out to start, do remove as much as you can from the room. The goal is to only allow what really belongs in that space to go back in.

Be sure to empty out long-ignored areas, like those baskets or bins hidden away in the back of a closet or the corner of the garage. If you are going to truly declutter, go for it all: closets, bins and boxes, drawers, cupboards, under your sink . . . you know where your clutter hides.

If you are not removing everything from a room all at once, empty one section at a time. Just clear one area and sort each item into one of four decluttering piles. (I talk more about these piles in just a bit.) Once you have finished with that section, move to the next, slowly working your way around the room. Clockwise or counter-clockwise, it doesn't matter. I typically pick a corner and start there.

Clean the Space

Take advantage of a cleared room to quickly clean the space. Vacuum those corners and carpeted areas that have been hidden by piles, boxes, or furniture. Shift the furniture and sweep or vacuum underneath it. Wipe down all the cleared shelves and dust as needed in the room, including a quick wipe-down of the baseboards that may have a layer of dust on them too.

Cleaning the area makes a big difference in your overall feeling about the space. It feels good to have an area clean and empty, and you'll be less likely to add clutter back into that space. You'll also be better able to imagine the possibilities of the space as well.

If you are planning something new for the room, then you will want to move furniture around or out before bringing back the items you've decided to keep. It's time to get excited, because you are creating a newly organized space, even if it's just the garage.

} A clean and organized space is a happy place.

Decide What Stays and What Goes

Once you have emptied the space, it's time to mindfully sort through everything and determine whether to keep it or get rid of it. This is really what decluttering is all about and is the most critical part of the process of getting organized. You also need to make sure everything that stays has a home. Everything in your house needs to have a permanent place where it belongs.

Be ruthless. Redistributing clutter is not getting rid of clutter, it is simply reorganizing it. If an item isn't useful or doesn't bless you, your family, or your home, then pitch it. When you come across things that you haven't used in a long time, be grateful it served its purpose and move on. Only allow back into a space things that you truly need and use.

> Keep reminding yourself that clutter interferes with your ability to manage your home—and it takes time to declutter again if you aren't ruthless during the first go-around.

Just as I use a four-leaf approach for prioritizing, I also break my decluttering down into four parts. Everything in the space you're decluttering needs to be placed into one of these four piles:

Keep Pile
Toss Pile
Blessing Pile
Sell Pile

I've been using this system for years. It's a quick and easy way to declutter any space. I typically use a few laundry baskets and a couple of trash bags to help me create my piles. Each basket gets a label (or a sticky note) with its category on it. Or you could just put note cards on the floor in four spots to distinguish which pile is which. The idea is to be able to go as fast as you can while you're clearing and sorting the room. The less guesswork, like which pile is which, the better.

The Keep Pile

Tools

I prefer to use a laundry basket for this pile so that I can easily carry things to where they belong within the room or around the house. If you have a two-story house, consider dividing your keep items into upstairs and downstairs piles. Sometimes I do this by putting upstairs items to the left in my basket and downstairs items to the right.

Tips

> Be brutal about what you keep. Keep only the best and most useful things.

> As you consider whether to keep an item or move it to another place, ask yourself these questions:
  - Is it a blessing to have in our home?
  - Do we still love it?
  - Do we still need it?
  - Do we still use it regularly?
  - Does it still work?
  - Does it fit?
  - Is it taking up too much space (think exercise equipment and old furniture)?
  - Could we live without it?
  - Does it reflect our current or new style (for clothes and decor)?

  There are plenty of other questions you can ask as you sort. But if this feels like too many questions, then just focus on the first few: *Do I love it, need it, or use it?* (Yes, you can also ask yourself if the item "sparks joy."*

*Kondo, *Life-Changing Magic of Tidying Up*, 41.

But deciding what you will keep goes beyond that. My plunger doesn't necessarily elicit joy, but we definitely need one in our home.) You don't have to say yes to every question, but they should help you determine if something is worth keeping. Move items that didn't make the cut to one of the other three piles.

> Take note of whether or not the item belongs in the room you're decluttering. It's possible that it might work better somewhere else, especially if it doesn't work with the function of the room. Simply set it in your keep basket to redistribute it to its proper location after you are done decluttering, not while you are still sorting. Stay focused on one room, then you can happily redistribute things once you're done.

> If the item doesn't have a "home," designate or create a spot for it. This is the most important task associated with the keep pile.

} If it's important enough to keep, then it's
} important enough to organize.

The Toss Pile

Tools

I prefer to use a large black trash bag or a trash can.

Tips

> Why a black trash bag? Well, because I don't want you second-guessing yourself, and I don't want your kids walking by and taking something out of the bag that you deemed as trash.

144

> It's great to declutter with kids, but if they're too young or easily distracted, do your decluttering without them.

> Again, be ruthless. Toss those dollar-store trinket treasures, broken toys, clothes with holes (that you never got around to patching), outdated food items and medications, any extra decor that is just cluttering your space, and those items that you never use and aren't worthy of being given away. I once heard these kinds of items described as "house dander." That's the perfect description. Get rid of it!

The Blessing Pile

Tools

I suggest a white trash bag (to distinguish it from the "toss pile"), another labeled basket, or a huge tub or bin. I keep a large bin in my garage for our donation items. If it's not already full of items to give away, I bring it into the room to declutter.

Tips

> Aside from your toss pile, this should be your biggest pile. Give, donate, and bless others with things that have been cluttering your home.

> You've probably heard it said, "One man's trash is another man's treasure." Remind yourself that you might be creating treasure for someone else with your never-used or no-longer-needed items, even if you're just taking them to your local donation center.

> Think through books you've already read, clothes you no longer wear, toys and games that haven't been played with in ages, and kitchen appliances or gadgets that seemed like a must-have at the time. Maybe a friend

145

would use your bread maker more than you. I recently found some kids' clothes that still had price tags on them. I had forgotten to return them and it was too late to do so. So I gave them to a girlfriend whose kids were younger. If you can't think of a friend who could use an item, take it to the Salvation Army or another donation center of your choice.

> I periodically ask our kids to go through their rooms to find toys to donate to other kids who may not have as many toys as they do. They usually get excited about the idea of helping others.

> Donating to some charities may qualify for a tax write-off with a receipt provided by the organization. Be sure to ask. I try to take a picture of my donation pile before I drop it off as documentation of my donation.

The Sell Pile

Tools

I prefer to use a laundry basket or bin for this pile.

Tips

> This is a dangerous pile! I usually start it intending to have a garage sale or to put the items up for sale online, but sometimes I don't get around to doing either. Usually I just move these items to my current blessing pile.

> Do you have any big-ticket items that you'd like to get some money out of? You could post them on social media (like on Facebook Marketplace) or offer them to friends and family at a huge discount. If the item doesn't sell, you may just need to decrease the price and post your ad again in a week.

> The most important thing is to give yourself a time frame for your sell pile—a deadline! If your "sell" items are still around at the end of this deadline, then this pile should be moved to your blessing pile and you may need to take another trip to your favorite donation center. You might also consider taking any gently used clothing items to a consignment or resale shop to see if you can sell them there.

Take Things to Their Proper Place

Once I've sorted everything into these four piles, I take my toss pile to the trash. I pack up my blessing pile for a trip to the Salvation Army and put any items I'm giving to friends in separate bags with their names on them. I snap pictures of each item in my sell pile before moving it into the garage. This way I already have photos for my ads. If I need to include the dimensions in the ad, I write those down too. I also put a deadline date on my calendar for when these items need to be sold—otherwise they get donated.

Next, I attack my keep pile. Items that belong in the room I'm organizing are returned to the room and put in their proper place. If I see a need for a new container or solution for the item, then I put it where it will go and make a note of its dimensions so I can find or purchase what I need to "give it a good home."

After I've made sure that everything in the room I'm working in has a home, I take any remaining items in the keep pile to whatever room they belong in.

TOOLBOX TIP

Organizing on a budget? Get creative with your storage containers and use what you already have around the house. Dollar stores are a great option for organizing on a budget too. They often have bins, baskets, and cute boxes that you can use to organize.

When You Have to Stop Mid-Decluttering

What if you have to stop mid-declutter, have piles everywhere, and are afraid your kids might move all your carefully sorted things around? If you have to stop earlier than expected—say, for example, your husband called and is bringing his bosses by the house—I recommend that you deal with each of the piles individually. Move your "keep" basket out of the room or into the corner of the room, and be sure to finish sorting through it when you have time. Toss your "trash" bag away. Put your "blessing" bag in the back of the car to take in the next time you run errands. Take your "sell" basket to the garage or wherever it will be stored until you can sell the items.

Even if you haven't completely finished decluttering the room, you've still put a dent in it. If you have moved everything out of the room because you expected to have more time to finish everything . . . well, you can create neat stacks of the items that still need to get sorted and finish later that day or the next day. Worst case, grab a little red wagon—I'm telling you, it's pretty handy!

Staying on Top of Paper Clutter

Staying on top of paper clutter is no easy task. Lots of people struggle with paper piles—including me. Here are my best tips on how to minimize the amount of paper in your home:

> **Go digital.** Go digital on as many lists and notes as possible. You can even scan documents and receipts that need to be kept. Use OneNote, Evernote, Dropbox, Asana, or other computer and phone apps to help get as much information stored digitally as possible. I use OneNote to keep all my important notes, lists, and ideas in one place. I have the app on my computer and on my phone. My lists sync between

my devices and can be shared with others—so my husband and I can both add things to our lists.

> **Pay bills online.** This will cut back on the paper coming into your home and, in some cases, allow you to automate some of your monthly tasks. Plus it saves money on stamps.

> **Set up a Brain Binder.** This is where I keep my master list, my current routine, and any other paper list that has my current to-dos. My Brain Binder houses all the paper that would otherwise end up on my counter. I'm a visual person and like to see what needs to get done (otherwise I tend to forget). Not a great thing if you or your spouse like clean counters. So I use my Brain Binder to house my paper lists, forms, notes, monthly calendar, and paperwork I need close at hand.

> I organize my paperwork using dividers that have pockets. This makes tucking away notes and paper fast and easy. Another tip is to keep a three-hole punch in your command center (see below) near your Brain Binder so you can quickly add things to your binder.

> **Create a family command center.** This is the area that houses all of your home office–type tasks—and hopefully most of your paper. Most command centers have baskets or mounted tiered files that act as an inbox for things like receipts, coupons, and sorted mail. Family calendars are often displayed in this space. Pencils, pens, tape, and basic office, mail, and bill-paying supplies are kept here as well. Many command centers have a chalkboard, cork board, or whiteboard for family members to write or post notes and reminders for each other. Consider doing a Pinterest search to get inspiration for how you can set up an attractive command center in your home.

> **Set up a filing system.** Get a file cabinet for your command center. Consider color-coding your files by category: financial files, household files, medical files, school files, family

files, fun files, lists, and so on. This allows you to quickly find what you are looking for. You know all those appliance manuals we all love to hold on to? I used to save them all in my file cabinet. Well, most appliance information can be found online, so feel free to trash those manuals. (It's a good idea to keep a file with all the serial numbers for your appliances and any service numbers or important information, but you can do this digitally by simply adding a tab or note for "appliances and devices" and then type in all the info you need stored.)

> **Set up a mail station.** Incoming mail is the source of many paper clutter headaches. My suggestion is to go directly to a trash can or recycling bin and toss out all junk mail right away. Next, open your mail and take immediate action on each item. You want to quickly categorize your incoming mail into piles. Here are a few "pile" ideas to get you started:

- *To pay.* Bills should be filed by due date in whatever bill-paying system you use. Be sure to write the due date for the bill on the top right (or left) corner of the envelope so you can easily keep track of when they need to get paid. Again, consider online bill paying.

- *To file.* File any mail that needs to be saved in the appropriate folder in your file cabinet. I like to keep my coupons filed in a portable coupon folder that I keep near my purse or in my car. Only keep coupons you know you'll actually use—not restaurants you *might* go to. Many coupons can be found online and printed before leaving the house, so you don't even need to save them. Look into getting store apps to take advantage of deals and avoid the need to clip coupons.

- *To respond.* Letters or other mail that requires action should go in this pile. Create a folder or inbox for such mail.

> ## TOOLBOX TIP
> Tear out pages and articles you want to save from magazines and catalogs and file them appropriately. This saves a ton of space. You can also take pictures and save the images in a folder in your digital note app.

- **To read.** Any letters, catalogs, or magazines you want to read need to have a place to be stored. If you are keeping them on a coffee table, create a limit for yourself so you know when it's time to recycle the older magazines. Cancel as many magazine subscriptions and catalogs as possible. Can you get that catalog online? Do you really love that magazine enough to have it in your house? Do you frequently use the tips or advice within it? I suggest having only one small basket to hold magazines and catalogs. If it starts to get full, then that's a reminder to throw away old copies you never read or finished.
- **Outgoing mail.** Outgoing mail is a bit easier to organize. Keep stamps, envelopes, and return address labels handy for outgoing mail. Establish one spot to put outgoing mail so that you know to take it to the mailbox.

YOU'VE GOT THIS!

Remember that it's easier to clear the clutter than to try to organize it constantly. It always feels good to remove the clutter, and being clutter-free makes for a more peaceful home environment. Decluttering can feel a little daunting when you first get started, but it's so rewarding when you are done. So go for it and get started!

Unlocking Joy

1. **Look at your calendar and pick a date to start decluttering.** Which room(s) or spaces are your top priority to get decluttered?

_____

_____

_____

2. **What do you struggle with most when you think about decluttering?** Is it finding the time? Getting started? Knowing you may need to get rid of things you're not ready to get rid of? Or maybe something else? Write down whatever comes to mind.

_____

_____

_____

Happy Decluttering!

13

Organizing Systems

Solutions for Getting Your Whole House in Order

It took every ounce of self-control for me to wait until this point in the book to share these strategies with you. But I knew the last thing you should do is create organizational systems with junk that you don't need in your house. Besides, since this is a book about organization, I figured it'd be nice if it were written in an orderly fashion. **Declutter first, then organize.**

Motherhood requires efficiency! We need to be able to smoothly get from one task to the next in the most effective way possible. In this chapter we'll look at methods for streamlining how you get work done and for properly storing your stuff to maximize your productivity. Toy organization will not be overlooked! And since we really enjoy entertaining in our home, I'm going to share a secret that will have my friends and family guessing where exactly I hide this system. You're going to love the order these tips can bring to your home . . . and you may even do a little shimmy as you read and get inspired to simplify your home.

Let's start exploring how you can create more efficiency throughout your home.

Ask Yourself a Few "Functional Organization" Questions

Whenever I'm organizing my own house or someone else's, I ask some functional organization questions. These questions help me determine the flow of the room I'm trying to organize and decide where things need to go. Adding pretty storage containers is great, but you need to have a game plan first.

> *How will each room be used?* Think through the activities that will be taking place in each room of your house. This may seem a little odd at first, but hang with me. Yes, you make food in your kitchen, eat at your dining room table, and probably hang out most in your family room. But you need to be specific about all that you do in each room as you start organizing it, because that will help you decide what goes where and what storage solutions you might need. For instance, if you normally play board games at the dining room table downstairs, then why would you store those games in an upstairs hall closet? If there is not a built-in storage area where you need one, then you may want to look into getting some sort of storage container for those games to keep them in or near your dining room. Do you enjoy baking more than cooking? Well, you'll want to make sure you have all your baking supplies stored in a more prominent place in the kitchen and organized in such a way that you can quickly gather what you need as you preheat your oven. Maybe a rollaway island stocked with your baking supplies would help you be more efficient.

> *What functions do I need this space for?* Taking the last question a step further, I try to determine how the space within the room can be used. If there is extra space in a bathroom to put a bench, I might turn it into a space to get ready in the morning and have all my makeup and hair supplies in that area. Does your guest room have space for a desk or hutch? Then consider turning a corner of the room into a much-needed office or craft area. When you have guests, you can just close the armoire doors and have a nice tidy room for them to relax in.

> *What items do I need to have handy in this space?* If school-work is done at a kitchen counter or table, you may want to consider storing anything needed for homework nearby. A basket or drawer with extra pens, pencils, erasers, and paper would be nice to keep in this area. A three-hole punch and stapler are also great to have close by, since work is often stored in binders and reports often need to be stapled. You may need an extension cord to make that space more computer friendly.

> *What are the problem areas in this room?* If things tend to collect in a certain spot, maybe it's time to find storage solutions for them or a better system for keeping that area clear. If you notice that you have a recurring issue in a room or area, then take some time to break down how the disorder is happening. Even if the answer is lazy kids (or parents . . . I get lazy too about putting things away), then updating the chore list or tweaking the routine may be the solution.

> *Do things in this room continue to be misplaced or not put away properly?* This is the story of our tape measure. It is constantly misplaced. It has a home, and everyone knows where its home is, but when projects are underway it often gets left on the floor or in random places. So we have had

to come up with solutions for this issue, like having a set place to lay tools when in the middle of a project. Our little rule is that all tools (and the tape measure) are put away as soon as the project is done or the day is over. We're less likely to misplace our tape measure when it's kept with other like items.

> *Where should items go?* You may be storing some of your belongings in random and less-convenient places instead of where you really need them. If you decide that items should be stored elsewhere, consider different storage options even if there isn't a place for them to be stored yet. Don't be afraid to create new homes for things you need stored in odd places with no obvious storage. A hook for keys near the door to the garage is a great example of this. Car keys should be kept near your car, so why not add storage for them? You don't need a table next to the door; you can simply mount a basket or a hook.

> *What do I use this area for most?* This is a similar question to figuring out the function of a space, but a bit different in that you may discover that the natural rhythm for a space is different than expected. Try to compartmentalize each room and think through what your family does in the space. Is your child drawn to sit and read near the window in the family room? Well, if that is what the space is getting used for, then why not make it more cozy? Consider adding a lamp or bean bag to that spot or rearrange the current furniture so that a comfortable chair or sofa is in that space to create a reading nook.

> *How can I be more efficient in this space?* Even once you've asked all the other questions, you still need to follow up by asking if you can use your space more efficiently. Regardless of the room or the specific area you are organizing, you may still be able to add another dimension of efficiency. We

use cinnamon so much in our home that I decided to buy a large, covered bamboo bowl to store it on the counter. It was a cute storage solution that meant my girls weren't climbing up my cabinets to get it from the spice cupboard for their morning oatmeal. (Don't get me started on how we had to repair a few cabinet doors after they used the knobs as leverage for scaling the counters.) This is also a great time to mention keeping things your kids use regularly within their reach. Anything you can do to help your kids be more efficient in doing things more independently, the better.

Categorize to Organize

Next, figure out what function an item serves. You are essentially looking for a theme or category for the things you use. This can take some practice, so here are a few ideas to get you started.

> **Kitchen categories:** cooking (pots, pans, cooking utensils), baking (Bundt pans, cupcake pans, 9 x 13 pans), food prep (knives, cutting boards), dishes, cleaning (under-sink supplies, hand towels), serving (pie server, ice cream scoop, other serving utensils), and restocking (extra paper towels, other products you store to replace ones in use).

> **Bathroom categories:** getting ready (makeup, hair-brushes, curling iron, hair dryer), cleaning, restocking

> ## TOOLBOX TIP
>
> Take inventory of each room as you organize it. Write down the basics of what is in each drawer and cupboard. You'll start to see themes as you go (first-aid items, serving utensils, meal prep necessities, chopping tools, and so forth). Make little notes about which items can be categorized together.

(toilet paper, soap refills, facial tissues), first aid (Band-Aids, medicine, cold remedies), jewelry, and towels.

> **Living or family room categories:** reading (books, blankets, extra pillows), games (cards, board games), furniture, entertainment (remotes, DVDs, music), and decor.

> **Toy storage categories:** toys with wheels, dolls, books, LEGOs. Maybe you will even divide toys by child, age, or gender.

> **Bedroom categories:** extra pillows or blankets, dirty clothes (hamper and lingerie bags), clean clothes (hanging areas and drawers).

Use Sticky Notes!

When it comes to organizing spaces, sticky notes are going to be your best friend. Use sticky notes as your guide to categorizing. Anytime I organize a room or area, I use two different colors of sticky notes and a permanent marker to determine

TOOLBOX TIP

The sticky note technique is great to use when organizing books. I store our books on shelves by categories. We have books on history, fiction, finance, parenting, marriage, homemaking, homeschooling, Bible studies, and more. As I'm sorting through our books and deciding which to keep, I think through what category the book would best fit in. Then I stack the books with sticky notes on the floor, so I don't forget how I'm grouping them. Once I've sorted through all the books and have taken the books I'm going to donate to the "blessing" bin, I dust the shelves and start putting sticky notes on the bookshelf to figure out the best way to organize our newly categorized books.

what I have (one color) and where the better place to store things might be (another color).

First, I use one color of sticky notes (say, orange) to write down the basics of what is in every cabinet and drawer. If there are multiple shelves in a cabinet, I use an orange sticky for each shelf and place it on the outside of the door. This way I'm able to get a quick visual of what I have in the space and where I've been storing things.

Next, I step back and look for common categories. As I'm figuring out categories, I write them on the other color sticky notes (say, blue). Then I stand back and try to determine where things should go. Which combination of cabinets, shelves, and drawers will house what I want together? After I've decided the new homes for things, I start placing my blue "category" notes on the outside of the area where things will be moved. If I notice that I'll need better storage, like a new drawer organizer or more bins, I jot it down on the sticky too.

Next, I move the orange "inventory" sticky notes to the appropriate blue sticky note location (the new home) one area at a time. Then, drawer by drawer, cabinet by cabinet, I move things around to their new homes.

My sticky note technique has even worked in major organization zones, such as when I completely reorganized my kitchen, dining room, and butler's pantry. I had serving plates, platters, and bowls in all those locations and wanted them all in consistent spots, so my kitchen and dining room cabinets were very colorful for a good solid week as I figured out the best way

TOOLBOX TIP

Christmas and birthdays are a great time to declutter and reorganize, since new toys and gifts are going to need space to be stored.

to categorize and organize those rooms. I decluttered as I went through each storage area too. I should add that it's helpful to leave a few sticky notes up on cabinets if you've dramatically changed where things are stored to help your family know where items are now residing. Of course, giving your family a little tour of your newly organized space is also a good idea.

Put Like Items Together

Once you have things categorized, think through where the best place to store each category will be. For example, in my laundry room I put things that belong together in bins to keep them organized. I have a bin for my drill that has the battery charger and all the drill bits inside as well. My electric sander bin not only has extra sandpaper circles but also stores safety glasses and dust masks. This way all the supplies I need for that one particular task are in one place. The key is not to have several locations for similar things throughout the house. **Part of bringing function into your home is keeping things you need or will use together in one well-thought-out spot.** This will save a ton of time in the long run.

Store Things Where You Will Use Them the Most

Where will you be using each item the most? Potholders should be stored in a drawer near the oven. I keep a container of toothpicks in this drawer as well, since I use toothpicks to check to see if my baked items are done. You want to be able to quickly access things when you need them.

This aspect of organization will be one of the most important to implement if you want your home to become more streamlined and efficient. This is a great practice to apply to your bathroom spaces too. Every bathroom in my house has the following cleaning supplies stored under the sink:

> Extra toilet paper: it's never fun to be the person who uses the last few squares of paper and needs more.

> Extra toiletries: I keep extra hand soap, shower supplies, and hand towels here as well. As we use the last "extra" I add it to my shopping list.

> Disinfectant wipes for cleaning up sink and toilet areas.

> Glass cleaner for wiping down mirror splatter.

> Toilet cleaner for keeping the toilet fresh.

> Toilet brush for those moments when flushing wasn't enough.

> Plungers for those normal plunger-required moments.

> Air fresheners, for obvious reasons, are nice to keep in bathrooms too.

Our powder room sink has a pedestal base, so we don't have "under the sink" space in there. However, I have a little cabinet I installed over the toilet that keeps most of these supplies handy. Baskets also work.

This is a huge timesaver since I don't have to go and get cleaning supplies if I see a mess that needs to be cleaned up (like "drips" around the toilet or gross stuff sticking to the side of the sink).

Establish "Stations" throughout Your House

I create "stations" for tasks I do on a regular basis. **A station is nothing more than a designated location for where work will be done.** The goal of creating stations is to create efficiency. For example, when we had babies in the house, I had a diaper-changing station. Counters make for great diaper-changing stations with the simple addition of a thick changing pad. I've used a hall counter, laundry room counter, and other open counter space. Just fill the drawer under the counter with all your diapering needs—or consider keeping a cute container full of supplies on the counter next to the changing pad. If you don't have a lot of counter space, no problem. You can keep all your changing supplies in a basket, including a small changing pad that can be folded, and take it to wherever you are changing your baby's diapers.

Another much-needed station in our house is a first-aid supply station. I used to keep all our first-aid supplies in our laundry room until I realized that the majority of the time my kids needed my first-aid skills was when they were playing in the backyard. So I moved my bin of Band-Aids, ointments, and sprays to a kitchen cabinet near the back of the house. I also keep a second stash of Band-Aids and some basic first-aid items upstairs in my bathroom cupboard. We seem to need Band-Aid "changes" upstairs after baths often enough that I just created a second little kit to save myself from running up and down the stairs at bedtime.

Add Labels for the Win

We've all seen those pretty closets and pantries with matching storage containers and fancy labels. If you have the budget for something like that, go for it. However, you can get any storage area looking great with just a simple label maker. You can even take your labeling to the next level by using chalkboard tags or stickers. Using a chalkboard pen will make your label last longer,

TOOLBOX TIP

Got sick kids? Keep a medicine station on the counter with all the medicines your kids have to take while they are sick. Have a notepad nearby to track the time meds are given to each child along with a note of when the next dose should be given. (Do make sure the medications on the counter have childproof caps.)

> ## TOOLBOX TIP
> Be sure to keep extra batteries and labeler tape cartridges ready to go if you are using a label maker. You don't want to come to a halt in your organizing just because you are lacking the right labeling supplies. It all circles back to "getting prepared" by having all the supplies you'll need in advance.

since they don't wipe off like normal chalk. I've also typed up labels, laminated them, and tied them onto baskets with some pretty ribbon to add a little dash of cute to my storage. There are vinyl labels that you can use as well.

Stay on Top of Toy Clutter

Nobody likes stepping on a toy airplane or LEGOs in the middle of the night. Toys can take over your house if you don't manage them wisely. Regardless of how many toys you have in your house, learning to store them properly is important for your mental health.

> The basic principle for toy management is that every toy in the house needs a "home"—and your child needs to know where that home is!

Get creative with how and where you store toys. Use baskets, bins, shelves, closets, and more for storage.

Staying on top of toy clutter starts with you. If you stay on top of things, you'll be able to teach your kids great habits for cleaning up as they grow (and their toy collection grows). **Teaching your children to be responsible for cleaning up their own toys and possessions is the most effective way to stay on top of toy clutter.**

In addition to making sure every toy has a home, consider a few of these tips:

> **Control the quantity.** Fewer toys equals less mess. That's obvious. Some families are perfectly happy keeping toys to a minimum. They are even able to keep all their family room toys in one basket. Since we have lots of kids at various ages and stages—and a combination of boys and girls—we have lots of different types of toys and several different baskets.

> **Designate areas for certain toys.** We have outside toys and inside toys. We also have upstairs toys and downstairs toys. We try to keep things in these general areas. However, I'm fine if my kids bring down a bin from upstairs to play with downstairs . . . as long as they take it back upstairs that night. You could also keep one or two baskets of toys in your family room and the rest in kids' rooms.

> **Rotate toys.** Kids can't play with every toy they have at the same time, despite their best efforts. We keep toys out that our kids play with most and store the rest in another room or closet. When they start to get bored with those toys, then we rotate them out with their other toys.

> **Label bins and storage clearly.** Sometimes kids don't know where to put their toys when they are done playing with them. Clearly labeled toy bins make for fast cleanup.

> **Create photo labels.** If your child is too young to read, then either draw a picture or snap a photo of the toys and create a label. Laminate the photo and stick it to the bin or attach it to a basket with ribbon.

> **Keep small toys separate.** Small toys can create big messes. Toys that are small or have tiny pieces also tend to get lost easily. Be sure to store small toys in bins with

lids and in hard-to-reach areas for toddlers. Plus, you don't want choking hazards lying around the house or in spots where little ones can pull them out.

> **Use a blanket to designate a playing space.** My kids know to grab a small blanket before they get LEGO projects or other small items out. It keeps the mess in one place and makes cleaning up easy.

> **Use metal baking pans for art supplies.** When my kids are playing with small beads or glitter, not only do they have to work at the kitchen counter but I also have them use baking pans with high edges. This keeps all the little bits and pieces in one, easy-to-clean spot.

Create "Grace Space": My Secret System!

I've given you a ton of tips on how to get rid of excess and manage your storage well, but we all know that when people come over we tend to sweep things off the counters and tuck them in any old place to make our house look clean and tidy . . . or at least cleaner and tidier. Well, that's just going to set you up for more chaos to undo later. If you've been trying to maintain order and then haphazardly shove things into a closet, drawer, or cupboard, you're really just shooting yourself in the foot. You don't want to create a mess where there wasn't one already.

That's why I have a designated "grace space." But what is it?

> Grace space is an intentional location to stick your excess and mess for those crazy moments when you need a space to look good quickly.

I'm not talking about the end of a long day when you are too tired to deal with the daily disarray. No! Your grace space is for those "Oh! My! Goodness! Are they already here?!" moments and the "So happy you stopped by" moments. Cue doorbell. Cue grace space.

What does grace space look like? Well, it might surprise you: your grace space should be a cute, covered container. Mine is a decorative basket with a lid. Now, here's the kicker: I want you to keep your grace space container in a room that you are in frequently. This is why I suggest you find something pretty to use. I want it to stare you down so that you will empty it out sooner rather than later. I don't want you to hide your clutter and forget about it. Yet, I totally get that there are just moments when you need to do a quick cleanup before your expected or unexpected guests arrive. Like I've said over and over again, I struggle with staying on top of the daily mess too. Grace space is my #momlife tip for those hospitality moments we find ourselves unprepared for.

YOU'VE GOT THIS!

There are so many different techniques you can use to get yourself and your family organized. Allow this section of the book to serve as a catalyst for ideas for your own home. Don't get overwhelmed by the number of tips and systems mentioned in this chapter or throughout this book. You don't need to do them all! Just pick a few that stand out to you and start implementing them. Try different variations or combinations and tweak them to work in your home.

Unlocking Joy

1. **Which room in your home is in most need of being better organized and more efficient?**

   _____

   _____

   _____

2. **What are three tips from this chapter that you want to start implementing?**

   _____

   _____

   _____

Storage Systems

Maximizing Your Storage Space

S torage is a tricky thing. On one hand, it's important to have a place to put seasonal items and important documents. On the other hand, we want to be wise about *what* things we are keeping and *where* we are keeping them. Sometimes we don't even need extra storage space; we just need less stuff. This is the exact reason why I suggest decluttering first. Once we've decided that something is worthy of our storage space, then we can turn our attention to where the best place would be to store it.

Whether you are struggling to find enough room to store things or you have enough space but simply need better storage solutions, the strategies I share in this chapter will help you figure out the most effective way to store your stuff.

Let's dive in!

Invest in Closet and Garage Organization Systems

Yes, it is possible to organize spaces without using fancy manufactured closet organizers. However, if it's in your budget, I recommend having a professionally designed storage system installed in your closets, pantry, or garage. Even doing this for only one of your storage spaces will be well worth it, believe me. If your master closet needs the most help, then go for it.

If you are going to invest in a garage system, be sure you know what you are going to store in there—and declutter first. Also, think through whether there are things in your house that might need to be stored in the garage in order to free up space inside. Hardware stores often sell organization systems that you design and put together. You might be able to save some money if you are skilled at projects like that.

Measure Your Space before Buying Containers

When you are getting ready to shop for new storage containers, consider how much will be stored (so you know the approximate size of container you'll need) and how big your space is (so you can find the perfect fit). You may be able to fit several baskets or bins on one shelf; just be sure to take into account how wide the shelf is as well as its depth and height. Yes, there is a little bit of basic math involved in organizing. Not too much, so don't be scared. Be sure to write down the measurements—and maybe even take a photo of the space to help you get inspired while you're out shopping for containers.

Store Clothes Efficiently and Creatively

It's funny to think about "storing" clothes, but that's essentially what we're doing in our closets, shelves, and drawers. We're storing our clean clothes until we wear them. Our current home has small bedrooms, so we've had to get creative with our clothing storage. Whenever storing clothes, either in a closet, in a dresser, on shelves, in baskets, or in bins, the first step is to determine how your clothes need to be stored: hung up (like suits and dresses) or folded (like T-shirts, jeans, socks, and underwear). Then you need to figure out how much of each type of storage space you'll need. My husband keeps his T-shirts folded on a shelf since the bulk of his hanging space is dominated by his suits and dress shirts, whereas I hang T-shirts since I have the space to hang most of my clothes. Since we both have different storage needs, we use our shelves, drawers, and hanging space differently.

As kids get bigger, so do their clothes; teens will require more storage space than younger kids. My teenage boys seem to be outgrowing their dressers and now hang up more of their clothes. If your kids are little and have trouble reaching the hanging bar in their closet, add a lower bar so they can access their clothes without help. Adding a lower bar also doubles your usable hanging space—that is, until your kids start wearing larger sizes and their clothes start hanging over the second bar. I'm telling you, growing kids complicate clothing storage!

Other solutions you may find helpful for storing clothing include:

> Behind-the-door shoe racks to store things like shoes, socks, leggings, and tights
> Hanging shelves added to closet rods for additional shelf space

TOOLBOX TIP

Store baby clothes by sizes and seasons. Your next baby may be born in a totally different season. Keep in mind that some little ones grow differently too. You may have a baby with lots of adorable, chubby rolls and another baby who is more petite. Proper labeling will help you know which clothes you may be able to use again with a new bundle of joy.

> Under-the-bed plastic bins with wheels for less frequently worn items
> Cute baskets set on top of dressers or even hung on the wall next to the closet
> Space-saving products such as hangers that have several bars for hanging multiple pairs of pants or skirts
> Clearly labeled bins in the garage, basement, or attic for seasonal clothing such as winter coats or ski clothes

Last, be mindful of just how many clothes you and your family members really need. Having fewer clothes to manage is easier than mountains of clothing that require lots of storage.

Be Selective and Creative When Storing Sentimental Keepsakes

Let me be clear: be very selective when it comes to storing sentimental items. If things are useful, then use them and enjoy the memories that go along with that keepsake. For instance, I love using my gram's rolling pin while making one of her pie crust recipes and remembering the wonderful times we enjoyed her pie together. That said, here are a few creative tips for your sentimental keepsakes:

> *Family shelf.* Display your family's antiques or special keepsakes on a bookcase shelf or in a curio cabinet along with a framed photo of the family member to whom they belonged. Kids will love seeing a picture of their great-great-grandma next to her teacup or serving dish. If you happen to have a photo of yourself as a child with that family member, frame that one.
> *Memory boxes.* When sorting through a child's baby clothes and paraphernalia, create a "memory box." You might in-

clude things like a few favorite outfits, some samples of your child's artwork, and some treasured love notes. Place these items in a clear bin with a cute 8 x 10 photo of the child inside the front. When your child becomes an adult, this can become a nice keepsake to pass along to them.

> *Art portfolio.* Select a few "favorite things" each year to store in an art portfolio that is divided by age or grade level. I have one for each of my kids. If a craft or piece of art is too large to store, I take a picture of it with the child who created it and store that in the portfolio. Most digital cameras track the date for the picture, which makes it easier to remember the ages of your children when they created their masterpieces. Plus, it's fun to see their sweet faces with their work. I've found that it also makes throwing things away much easier.

Make the Most of the Space You Have

There are so many simple space management techniques that can be used throughout your home and in just about any room. Here are some ideas on how you can best maximize the storage spaces you already have within your home.

> **Think inside the drawer.** Any drawer can quickly turn into a crazy junk drawer. Use drawer organizers, small boxes, and containers to clearly distinguish storage. This will help keep things organized. I've found that plastic food storage containers that have lost their lids can be repurposed for keeping drawers tidy.

> **Think outside the box.** You don't have to use clear plastic containers for storing things on shelves. I love adding texture and some style by using cute baskets, bins, boxes, mason jars, and more. Head over to your local craft store to get ideas for the types of things you can use for storage.

Cute storage containers can be left out and displayed versus being tucked away in a cupboard.

> **Use counter space—carefully.** Counters are a magnet for clutter. I recommend saving your counter space for your most-used appliances and for simple kitchen and bathroom decor. Try to find different "homes" for other household appliances and knickknacks so you can keep your counters as clear as possible.

> **Use the space under beds and furniture.** The space under couches and beds works great for storage. I keep our extra dining room table leaves and pads under our guest room bed. My kids have rolling bins for storing toys and their keepsakes under their beds. I even store my laptop lap pad under a couch. If you have a bench in your kitchen, you might be able to fit a few baskets underneath to store extra tablecloths, place mats, or cloth napkins. (This works best when the bench is pushed up against a wall, so the baskets don't get kicked into your kitchen space.)

> **Maximize shelf space.** Add stackable or tiered shelves to a cupboard to get more use out of it. A lazy Susan is one of my favorite ways to create more usable space in cabinets and on shelves in the pantry, refrigerator, cupboards, and more.

> **Find functional furniture.** I know that may sound a little odd. Not every piece of furniture in your house has to be functional or have more than one purpose. A cute, comfortable couch is a good thing. Cute and comfortable count as two functions in my book. But if you can find furniture that has extra storage inside—bonus! Piano benches, coffee tables, side tables, footstools, and more are often designed with built-in storage.

> **Save your best storage spaces for your most-used items.** If you use something daily, store it where you can easily access it. It'd be crazy to store your measuring cups on a

high shelf in the pantry if you use them frequently. Snow jackets don't need to take up space in your hall closet if you live in a warm climate and only go skiing once a year. High shelves and the back of cabinets and cupboards should be used for things that you don't need as often. For instance, I store extra pillows and blankets on the highest shelves in our linen closet. This type of space is also a great place for storing kitchen appliances that don't get used very regularly.

> **Use wall space and door space.** Never overlook the potential of wall space, even in the kitchen. You can use hooks, baskets, open shelving, magnetic strips, and even pegboards on your walls to add storage and function. Don't forget that you can add storage behind doors and on the inside of cabinet doors too. If your space is limited, properly utilizing these two areas may be the perfect solution you've been looking for.

> **Consider pegboards.** Pegboards are growing in popularity these days. They have been widely used for garage organization for years and are now making their way to the kitchen. I've seen kitchen pegboards pop up on home shows, blogs, and all over Pinterest. The basic concept is to install a large board that has predrilled holes spaced evenly across its surface and add various-sized shelves, hooks, and baskets for storage. What's great with this system is that it's easy to adjust the pegs to create new storage space for the containers you want to use next. You may even want to consider putting one up in your pantry or command center.

> **Use your ceiling space.** Hang pots and pans near your stovetop with a cute pot rack. Many pot racks even have a shelf on top to stack other pots. Ceilings can also be used to hang other storage solutions, such as macramé hangers that hold baskets or pretty ceramic bowls in order to keep things close to where they can be used. Hanging storage also

works great in closets and even in bedrooms for clothes, toys, and stuffed animals. Overhead storage is a must in garages. If you can't get shelving units installed on your garage walls, then consider overhead storage.

> **Utilize storage on wheels.** You can pick up shelving units on wheels at most warehouse stores. These are great for storing bins and lots of different things in your garage, pantry, or even outdoor spaces (if they're weather-resistant). They come in all shapes, sizes, and styles. Some even have a hanging rod for storing seasonal clothes. Don't forget about adding rolling storage to your kitchen too, such as a kitchen island on wheels, which can be rolled out when you need it or kept stationary for more permanent use.

> **Use the space under your upper cabinets.** Hooks can be used to hang mugs under a cabinet near your coffeemaker to create more storage. If your mugs are cute or even seasonal, they'll add some extra charm to your space too. Magnetic strips attached under cabinets are great for storing spices in metal containers.

———— YOU'VE GOT THIS! ————

Having the right things stored the right way is an important part of getting organized. You don't have to settle for ordinary storage solutions. You can implement beautiful and functional storage containers to create a lovely, welcoming, less cluttered environment in your home. Be intentional with what you decide to store and get creative.

Unlocking Joy

1. What areas of your home need better storage?

_____

_____

_____

2. What storage solutions might work best for that space?

_____

_____

_____

15

Chore Systems

Training Kids to Help

I may get a few eye rolls from my teens, but my younger kids still think it's funny when I attempt to cheer them on in the mornings as we do chores with my little rally cry, "Go Team Clover!" Maybe I'm having some sort of a flashback to my short career as a cheerleader in the eighth grade. But in our house it's "all hands on deck" when it's chore time. If you can walk without falling over and recite at least a few letters of your ABCs, then you are fair game to be assigned a chore. In our minds, managing our home is a team sport. So we train our kids to help with basic housecleaning, tidying, and even organizing. Kids are natural mess makers, but they can also be incredible helpers—even when they're young. We encourage teamwork and expect everyone to pitch in and help when it's time to do chores.

There are many ways to create a system for chores, and in this chapter I'll introduce you to a few of my favorites. These chore systems may work fabulously for some families but require a few adjustments to work well for others. Just keep changing things up to see what works best for your family. Every six months or so, you may need to modify your chore systems, especially as your kids get older and are able to do more. Just remember to let go of perfectionism during the training process! And keep reminding yourself that you're teaching your kids important life skills as they learn new jobs to do around the house.

Tips for Chore System Success

Before we jump into ideas for specific chore systems, here are a few things to consider when putting together your chore routines and systems.

Figure out what chores need to be done regularly and how often. This overlaps with what we discussed in chapter 7 about creating routines, because chores should be built into your family's routine and schedule. This involves:

> Creating a list of all the chores you'd like to have done around the house.

> Breaking those chores down by what needs to get done daily, weekly, biweekly, quarterly, and annually. If necessary, refer back to chapter 7 for ideas about which chores to get done daily, weekly, and biweekly. A few of my family's quarterly chores include wiping down ceiling fan blades, baseboards, doors, marks on walls, and other odds and ends that can't wait a full year to get done. Annually, we scrub the grout in our main living areas using old toothbrushes and a bowl of warm soapy water. (This is actually a favorite chore in our house.) Other annual chores include decluttering kids' rooms and closets. We do this more frequently if I notice that piles are growing in corners.

> Making a note of which day each weekly chore needs to be done. Keep in mind that this list may include jobs your kids are not yet ready to learn. That's fine. You can pick a few to get them started and keep adding new skills through the years.

Rotate chores. As you train your kids to do various jobs, consider rotating chores among them. This may be hard to do if you have younger kids and older kids in the mix. But if you have kids of similar ages or capabilities, rotate responsibilities from time to time so that everyone is learning to do all the jobs in the house. If you have one child, then consider switching out the jobs this child does so he or she can continue to learn new tasks—or have your child rotate with you. Rotating jobs helps kids appreciate all the hard work everyone else has been doing as they take on the same task.

Some families rotate jobs throughout the week. This gets a little too confusing for my family. We tend to keep the same jobs for several months and then switch. My younger kids will sometimes be assigned to assist an older sibling. There are often little things that they can do to help with a job. It's fun to see my kids working together to get chores done.

Apply the "first this, then that" rule. It's much easier to get kids to tidy up or get a few chores done *before* we give them privileges like getting to watch a show, play on an electronic device, hang out with friends, or eat dessert. Kids are naturally motivated by fun, so we've implemented the "first this, then that" rule. It's

TOOLBOX TIP

Consider training your kids to do new chores during the summer months. Life is usually a bit slower then, and more time can be taken to teach them how to do new jobs.

pretty straightforward. When my kids ask to do something fun, I'll simply look around to make sure they've done their chores and that the house is tidy. If not, I ask them to first do those things before they can have or do what they are asking for. My hope is that eventually they'll realize they should check to see if everything is actually done before they come and ask for a privilege.

Have visual reminders. It's helpful for kids to have visual reminders of what chores they need to do and what those chores involve. Whether this is done by a checklist, chore board, or even a photo of the area that needs to get cleaned, I find that jobs are more likely to get done properly when my kids have a visual prompt.

Create some sort of accountability. When you hold your kids accountable for finishing the work assigned to them, they are more likely to do it. So it's important that you come up with a way for your kids to "sign off" or let you know when they finish a job. You could run around the house doing room checks, but that just adds an extra chore for you to do each morning. I tried doing this for a while, and let's just say it didn't work well. Most of the time I was busy trying to get my own to-dos done and forgot to check up on completed kid jobs throughout the house. When I didn't consistently check to see if they'd gotten things done, it created complacency with some of my kids. They got used to me not following through and just waited until they were told to get something done. Now all my chore systems include some sort of "visual" for me to see that they have completed their work. Sometimes it's a checkmark on a checklist or moving a magnet or clip to a "done" area. Whatever chore system you decide to try, make sure your kids have a spot to indicate that they finished their chores.

Have clear expectations. I've also learned the importance of being clear about what my expectations are regarding each chore. This applies more for my older, more capable children. For example, if someone is responsible for taking care of the dirty dishes, my expectation is that they look around to see if there are any dirty pots or pans left on the stovetop or dishes left on the kitchen island or table. If wiping down counters is the task at hand, then I clearly explain which counters I expect to be included in that chore. Sometimes I write out details for the assigned chores so my kids can reference what all each one includes. I've done this on index cards (as I'll explain in a bit) and on a chore list that I used to have hanging on the inside of a kitchen cupboard.

Simplify your cleaning tools. Use tools that make chores easier to do from start to finish. For example, I keep a cordless vacuum mounted in the kitchen area—which my kids actually like using—so that I don't have to get out our big vacuum. It's great for quick cleanups. We also use a disposable duster rather than getting out spray cleaner and a rag. First, my kids think it's fun to use the disposable dusters. Second, I like that the disposable dusters attract dust and don't just sweep it into the air. Old socks work great as cleaning rags too. We also use a soap-filled kitchen brush that makes washing dishes a snap. Any cleaning tool that cuts out an extra step is a welcome addition to our cleaning arsenal.

Keep the right tools in the right places. This is essential for setting kids up for success. I keep everything my kids need to do their cleaning chores in a red bucket under the laundry room sink. I stock it with all-natural cleaning spray, glass cleaner, a disposable duster, an extra toilet brush, and kitchen gloves. I've found that my kids don't complain quite as much when they can wear gloves to clean toilets and other messes they deem gross. The cleaning bucket sits right next to the basket of rags, so my kids can grab as many rags as they need for the job.

Creating Chore Systems

A simple search of "chore systems" on Pinterest will show you more ideas than you could ever dream of trying out. So instead of overwhelming you with too many choices, I'll share a few systems we've used that might work well in your home too.

The Chore Board

We use this system the most. I have a massive magnetic chalkboard hanging in the hallway near our kitchen where I post all the chores that need to be done throughout the week. You could also use a whiteboard or a poster board. Really anything could work. In years past, I laminated and posted my kids' chore lists on the inside of a cupboard. However, now that we have more kids (and more chores to distribute), I prefer using my large, pretty chalkboard.

Before I write anything on this chore board, I decide which chores I want each kid to do using the list of chores I've created. Next, I assign weekly and daily chores to all the kids, making sure the jobs are as evenly distributed as possible. Once our family has talked over who will do which chore, I'm ready to post their assignments on the chalkboard.

Using a white chalkboard pen, I write the word *weekly* along with the days of the week across the top of the board. Under each day, I make note of everyone's laundry day as well as any weekly chores they are to do. Since I have a large family, I use a different colored chalkboard pen for each family member. This helps them to quickly identify their jobs. On the left-hand side of the board, I list all of the chores to be done *daily* along with the name or initials of the person responsible for the chore. I write "All" next to those chores that all of us are supposed to do. I also note if a daily chore is a morning or evening job.

Why magnetic? you may wonder. Well, this allows me to add little magnets to the board that the kids use as a way to indicate that they have completed their chores. These days I rarely have to make changes to our chore board. I only switch out the names listed next to the chores. With a little bit of spray cleaner, I carefully wipe off one child's name and write in the new assignee.

Clipboard Checklists

Another fairly straightforward method is to give each child their own clipboard along with their weekly chore list tucked under the clip, or use one master clipboard for all of your children's weekly chore lists.

To create the checklist, write out all the chores that each person needs to get done every week. Make a note of when chores are to be done: mornings, evenings, or on certain days of the week. I suggest typing up a master checklist for each child so that you can easily print off new lists as you need them. It's helpful to print each child's checklist on different colored paper so your kids can easily tell them apart. You can also laminate the list and have your kids use a dry erase marker to check things off as they go. Plastic sheet protectors work great if you don't have access to a laminator.

Chore "Sticks"

The chore stick system is easy, and kids typically love it. Write out each chore on a craft stick—one chore per stick. Then give each child a jar containing all the sticks with chores assigned to them. Be sure to use the large sticks—actually, they are tongue depressors, but I didn't want to call them "chore depressors." That just sounds weird! You can get large craft sticks at most craft stores. On one end of the stick you can put colorful washi tape. When chores are completed, your child can put the stick back in the jar with the washi side up. This makes it easy to see which chores are done and which are not.

Here are a couple of ideas to make this system work more smoothly:

> Use different colored washi tape to differentiate if the chore is a daily chore or a weekly chore, or have a different color for each day of the week. Personally, I would go

in the order of the rainbow, then add a little index to the outside of the jar using the tape.

> Add a small picture or drawing of the chore on the stick for pre-readers.

Custom Dry Erase Boards

Chances are you've seen examples of this kind of chore chart. The best dry erase boards are those that have the days of the week across the top and blank spaces to write in the chores that need to be done on the left-hand side. The most efficient way to use these boards is to write in the child's name next to the chore and to leave a spot for them to check off completed work. This is a great system to use if you are thinking about having your kids switch off chores throughout the week. This is a visual way for them to see *who* is doing *what* each day. For those tasks that need to be done by all your kids or by more than one child, have your kids use different colored dry erase pens to add their personal checkmark to the box.

Index Card Boxes

I'm pretty sure that the first system I used to manage my home involved an index card system. To use this system, write each chore on an index card. (You can cut back on the number of cards used by listing all the "morning chores" on one card.) Store all the cards in a recipe box with a divider for each child's name. Put each of your children's chore cards in the section assigned to them. Be sure to label or color-code each index card to indicate if the card is for daily work, weekly work, and so on. If the card is an annual card, at the top of the card write the month the job should be done. This will help with keeping your cards organized.

For smaller kids, put a photo of the chore to be done on the card as an indicator of how the area should look when they've completed their work. Once they're finished with each chore have them turn the card around and place it back in the box behind their tab. Play with this system to see how you can get it to work for your family.

Chore Packs

Basically, chore packs are comprised of photo cards or index cards with chores listed on them. Each child has his or her own large plastic name tag holder with a pouch for storing chore cards and a lanyard attached to it. This way your kids can put their pack of chores around their necks and go about the house completing their assignments card by card. Once they have completed all their chores, they can hang up the chore pack. I'd recommend hanging your chore packs using a stick-on hook in a discreet area in your kitchen, like the inside of a cupboard or near your pantry. My tweak to this system would be to use it in combination with the index box system. This way you can change out weekly chores and have a place to store chore cards not being used on a particular day. Another idea for this system is to create a mini chore chart (or checklist) for each person with a picture of the chore, then laminate it and attach it to the lanyard with a binder ring. This would mean they have only one card attached to the lanyard. The drawback here is that it's not as easy to update and make changes.

The Daily Mess: My Whiteboard Solution

Chores systems are great, but messes still collect throughout the day: clothes lying all over the bedroom floor or stuffed under the bed, dishes left on the counter, schoolwork spread out everywhere—the list could go on and on. Some kids are naturally neater than others. For the not-so-tidy kids, it's important to come up with a system that holds them accountable for picking up after themselves.

Here's a solution that works well for our family: if I notice that a child didn't do something I'd asked them to do earlier in the day, I pull out a small whiteboard I keep tucked away in my kitchen and write down their name along with the task that needs to get done. Then I set the little whiteboard on the counter where everyone will see it. *To be clear, this is not the same chore board I mentioned earlier.* You don't even need to use a whiteboard; you can use a sticky note or a piece of paper. However, I like that the whiteboard is easy to reuse and is hard to miss, making it obvious that Mom or Dad discovered something that needs to get done. The entire household can see what tasks are undone and who is responsible for doing them. Instant accountability.

I've been amazed by how much this eliminates stress for me. Normally, I'd just get frustrated when something was repeatedly forgotten or when I'd discover something left undone and the child was not around to ask to complete the job. I get tired of sounding like a broken record. With the whiteboard, I no longer have to remember to remind a child "again" and make sure the job gets done. It's written down and I can free up my brain to think about things other than remembering who needs to do what.

One sidenote here is that our kids are allowed to put a checkmark next to their completed jobs but not wipe it off the board. I am the only "master eraser," because I want to be able to double-check that the job actually got completed properly.

YOU'VE GOT THIS!

When we teach our kids to help keep our homes clean and tidy, we are imparting important life skills to them. More often than not, they are the main culprits for much of the mess in the house. So why not train them to be responsible for helping around the house? Plus, I've noticed that my kids have a sense of pride when our house is in order before we have friends and family over. My girls love to take people upstairs to see their tidy room. Make a list, pick a system to try, and *get your worker bees buzzing.*

Unlocking Joy

1. **Make a list of all the daily and weekly chores that need to get done around your house.**

   ☐ Done!

2. **What chores would you like to see your kids start learning?**

   _____

   _____

   _____

3. **Which of these chore systems do you want to try?**

   _____

   _____

   _____

* Want to see these chore systems in real life? My website has blog posts and videos that show more detail about them. Head over to **KristiClover.com/Home** to check them out or just type "chore systems" into the search bar on my site.

16

Kitchen Systems

Organization and Meal Planning Systems

The kitchen is one of the busiest rooms in most homes, so it's important to build as much order and efficiency into how we use it as possible. Got a small kitchen? No problem. In this chapter we'll be looking at how to bring function to even the most oddly designed kitchen.

You'll be surprised just how many creative ways there are to utilize space in your kitchen and eating areas. We'll talk about how to build efficiency and order into your kitchen and close with a helpful section on meal planning.

Organizing Your Kitchen Using "Stations"

Most homes aren't designed with organization or efficiency in mind. Unfortunately, this is the case with my kitchen. It's beautiful, but its "work triangle" is more like a crazy ninja star (an efficient kitchen space should have the sink, refrigerator, and stovetop close together in somewhat of a triangle formation with counter space in between). In order to make my kitchen more efficient, I've created stations. My kitchen stations are simply designated areas where specific tasks are performed.

You've probably seen cooking shows where they have everything premeasured and ready to go for their cooking demonstration. This is actually called *mise en place* in the cooking world. I just learned this term in an online cooking class. It's French and is translated as "everything in place." Of course, my snarky side wants to translate it as keeping your "mess in its place." Now, don't get me wrong; I'm not saying you have to have everything premeasured before you start throwing your meals together. What I am suggesting is that you keep all the tools you'll need for a specific task in a designated "station" in the kitchen. This way you aren't wasting time running around your kitchen to find things when you're trying to get a meal on the table.

Depending on the size of your kitchen, you may need to use an area for several tasks (or maybe all tasks if your kitchen is small). That still works; just be sure you know *where* you will do *what* and organize things accordingly. Ideally, all the tools associated with a specific task would be stored near the station. If that isn't possible given your kitchen, I recommend putting the tools you'll need in a bin or basket that you can move to the station when you are performing that task. I use removable organizers in my kitchen drawers so that I can grab whichever little in-drawer basket of tools I need and get to work.

Here are the stations I've created to build efficiency in my kitchen.

> **Meal prep station.** Designate a specific area in your kitchen where you will do all your meal prepping: chopping, measuring, and mixing. I usually prep my meals next to my stovetop, since I cook the majority of our meals on it. Tools that should be stored close to this area include cutting boards, knives,

mixing bowls, and measuring cups and spoons. Be sure to grab all the ingredients that you'll be using for your meal before you get started too.

> **Cooking station.** Obviously, this is your stovetop or the counter space where you have your crockpot, instant pressure cooker, rice cooker, or whatever cooking device you may be using. If possible, store your pots, pans, and cookware near this station. Before you start cooking, pull out everything you'll need for your meal and have the items ready for use. Since you will need access to your salt, pepper, spices, oils, and any sauces you might be adding as you cook, I recommend storing these items as close to your stovetop as possible. I store my salt and pepper in covered bamboo bowls right next to my stovetop and have my spice cabinet right behind my cooking area. I also keep a crock filled with my most-used cooking utensils on the counter next to the stovetop.

> **Baking station.** I have designated drawers in my kitchen where I keep my tools and supplies for baking. My stand mixer sits on the counter next to my flour and sugar canisters. All my measuring cups and spoons are in a small bin inside one of my drawers. I just pull out the bin and move it to the space I'm using to do all my measuring.

> **Dish-cleaning station.** It goes without saying (but I'm going to say it anyway) that this station is your kitchen sink and the counter area next to it. I keep a clean sponge and soap-filled

---

TOOLBOX TIP

Keep a "junk bowl" handy as you prep your meals. This is just an extra bowl to keep on your counter to toss all your eggshells, peels, scraps, wrappers, and the "junk" you will be throwing away. This saves you from walking back and forth to the trash and keeps your prep area clean.

brush on my counter for easy meal cleanup. It's helpful to keep all your dishwashing supplies (and other quick cleanup supplies) in the cupboard under the sink. Here are a few things you'll find under my kitchen sink:

- Dishwashing supplies: dish soap, dishwasher detergent, extra sponges, and brush replacements for my soap-filled brush
- Scouring pad and small plastic food scraper for tough, baked-on food
- Scouring powder (such as Bar Keepers Friend) for cleaning pots and pans and making the kitchen sink sparkle
- Disinfectant wipes (such as Clorox) for disinfecting counters and floors
- Extra rags for cleaning up spills and messes
- Carpet cleaner for quickly getting messes out of rugs and carpeted areas near the kitchen

TOOLBOX TIP

Have a dishwashing system—and make sure everyone in your home knows what it is. It's important for everyone to have a basic understanding of how to handle the clean and dirty dishes in your home. For example, do you have two sides to your sink? If so, decide if both sides are for dirty dishes or if you'll use one side for air-drying clean dishes. In our home, the right side of the sink (that has the garbage disposal) is where we scrape dirty dishes and the right counter area is where we stack the dirty dishes after dinner. The left side of the sink and the left side of the counter are for clean dishes. My kids who can't reach the higher cabinets to put away clean dishes when they are emptying the dishwasher know to put those dishes on the drying pad on the "clean" side of the counter.

- Basic cleaning spray for normal day-to-day cleaning and wiping down counters
- Glass cleaner for water splashes on windows
- Disposable duster for quick dusting of shelves, top of the refrigerator, and more

> **Storage station.** Designate a drawer or cabinet in your kitchen where you will store all the containers and their lids for your leftovers. I typically stack the containers inside each other as best as I can and then keep all the lids together. I keep my plastic wrap, foil, and resealable plastic bags in a separate drawer. The state of our container drawer depends on the person who is putting the containers away. If you only have space on a lower cupboard shelf for your storage containers, consider getting a bin that you can use like a drawer. This will make it easier to access all your containers to find the right size for the job.

> **Beverage station.** I've created a beverage station in my butler's pantry area next to the kitchen. I have a drawer filled with a variety of teas. I keep my coffeemaker on the counter with a swivel stand for my coffee pod selections. I use small glass bowls to hold sugar packets and honey sticks. I even keep a little basketful of hot chocolate packets. All of our mugs and teacups are in this area too. We also have a mini refrigerator here that we keep stocked with sodas, sparkling waters and juices, and sports drinks for friends to enjoy.

TOOLBOX TIP

What if there is little space in the refrigerator for all the leftovers (like after a holiday meal)? I sometimes stick leftover food into resealable plastic bags. They're great space savers.

> ### TOOLBOX TIP
>
> Tea parties are a great way for your kids to practice good table manners. When I'm feeling fancy, I bake scones and get out the lemon curd. However, most days I keep it simple and serve tea with sliced fruit and some sweet crackers—or, should I say, "biscuits."

Organizing Your Cupboards, Pantry, Refrigerator, and Freezer

It's easier to stay on top of the food you have in your cupboards, pantry, refrigerator, and freezer when you designate areas for similar foods to be stored—plus, your family knows exactly where to check before opening a new bag or jar of food.

Think of these storage spaces like a miniature grocery store. There is a cereal aisle, canned good aisle, baking supply aisle, and so on. When organizing your own grocery shelves and spaces, keep these "aisles" in mind. Essentially, you're organizing food by category and packaging. My refrigerator has designated spaces for dairy products, leftovers, breads, fruits, vegetables, and condiments. My freezer has designated sections for meats, fruits, vegetables, frozen meals, easy lunch options, and desserts. I keep my baking supplies, such as large bags of flour and sugar, baking powder, baking soda, cocoa powder, powdered sugar, and such in one area in my pantry.

Don't forget to add lazy Susans to your pantry, refrigerator, and cupboards to maximize space and create easier access to all that is being stored. Building efficiency into these storage areas sometimes requires a little creativity, especially if your kitchen design is less than functional. Here are some additional ideas to help you out.

Use my sticky note technique. Figure out the best storage and flow for organizing your kitchen cupboards and cabinets using the easy sticky note technique that I introduced in chapter 13. Actually, much of the advice in that chapter can be applied in your kitchen.

Keep the kids' dishes where they can reach them. If you can spare the space, store dishes low enough for kids to get to them. We have a shelf in our kitchen where we keep all the kids' less-breakable dishes, bowls, and cups. It makes it easy for them to get breakfast for themselves and snacks throughout the day—and to help set the table. I also have a large, cute bin filled with Mom-approved snack foods on a low shelf in my pantry.

Keep your most-used kitchen tools front and center. Store rarely used kitchen tools and serving platters on high shelves, in the back of cupboards, or even in the garage or basement if only used a few times per year. This same rule applies to kitchen counters. We use our blender and toaster oven every day, so they stay on the counter. However, other kitchen appliances get stored away until I need them, like my waffle iron, crockpot, and bread maker.

Label! Label! Label! You don't have to label the inside of every cupboard and drawer, but there are times it may be helpful. I

TOOLBOX TIP

Keeping water glasses from taking over and multiplying can be a full-time job. We use a few different systems for our cups, glasses, and water bottles. My favorite involves using mason jars as our water glasses. I add different washi tape to each person's jar and write their name on the tape. This helps us to know whose jar is whose and cuts back on people continuing to pull out new glasses when they're thirsty. When we have guests visiting or we are on vacation, I use sticky notes as placeholders for each person's glass.

Of course, if you are using plastic cups for a party, then permanent markers are perfect for writing names on cups.

store my juicer, ice cream maker, other large appliances, and serving pieces in high cupboards and sometimes in the back of cabinets, and I add labels to those shelves to remind myself what is stored there.

When we had our friends living with us a couple of years ago, I went as far as to label the inside of the refrigerator. I knew where I wanted things to go, but no one else did. The day I found three peanut butter jars, two ketchups, and three applesauce jars open in the refrigerator was the day that I pulled out my label maker and got busy. My pantry baskets and bins get labels too.

> When you label shelves in your pantry, freezer, and refrigerator, it allows everyone in the house to know where things go—and see if there is really need for a new container to be opened.

Take inventory in your freezer at least twice a year. Food can quickly be forgotten when lost in the depths of a freezer. I often add a note to my calendar to get this project done before freezer burn ruins our food. As I'm pulling things out, I write down what

TOOLBOX TIP

I have a large whiteboard hanging in our pantry that we use to write down whatever items we need or whatever has been used up. I used a permanent marker to create store categories across the top of the board: a couple grocery stores, a warehouse store, a merchandise store, a craft store, and a home improvement store. I mounted a basket with dry erase pens next to the board to make it easy for everyone to jot down anything we need to buy. When I'm putting together a grocery list for the week, I take note of anything that was added to the whiteboard.

> ## • • • • • • • • TOOLBOX TIP • • • • • • • • •
>
> When defrosting meat and freezer meals, always put your frozen items in a large bowl to thaw. Regardless of whether you are using your kitchen counter or the refrigerator, the last thing you want is to have a bloody or goopy mess to clean up as it defrosts.

I have in stock and try to do a little meal planning at the same time (or right after I'm done).

One system I use to track our freezer food is to hang my freezer inventory list in my pantry along with my meal planning ideas. When I sit down to figure out our week's meals, I check my freezer list to see what I can add to the menu. Another idea is to use a dry erase marker to write all the food stored on each shelf and in each bin on the inside wall of my freezer. This system works well for our garage side-by-side freezer. However, it doesn't work for my large freezer drawer inside our house.

One drawback to most freezer organization systems is that you have to remember to add new items you purchase to the list. This is why I frequently plan "let's use up what we have in the freezer" weeks. I typically do this whenever my freezer is looking full or when I've done one of my big freezer inventories.

Don't forget to regularly declutter your kitchen! Get rid of old, broken, or duplicate items at least once a year. Regularly check your pantry and refrigerator for expired food. I do this every week as I'm putting away my groceries. Most leftover food won't last much longer than a week, so make sure you create a routine for cleaning out your refrigerator regularly. Also wipe down the shelves as needed to keep your refrigerator looking great (and sanitary). If you tend to forget to clean out your refrigerator or had to put food away fast, I suggest marking your calendar to remind yourself to get it done. Don't allow the foods in your fridge to become science experiments.

Tried-and-True Systems for Hassle-Free Meal Planning

If you are not a believer in your need to meal plan, or if you feel like a failure at it—oh my, you are in for a treat. I'm going to make it easy. You don't even have to like to cook! I'm a big believer in planning ahead for easy meals. I try to keep my freezer and pantry stocked with ingredients that I can just throw together to make a meal. These are the sanity-saving meals for those nights when I'm not in the mood to cook or haven't made it to the store yet.

Through the years I've developed several different systems for meal planning, and what follows is an overview of each of them.

My Recipe Binder System

Most people have some combination of recipe books and boxes, magazines with dog-eared corners, and printouts from recipe websites that float around the kitchen, which makes it hard to find a particular recipe. Besides, it's difficult to organize recipes when they come in so many different forms and sizes.

One year, I decided to create my own system for organizing my recipes: my recipe binder system. First, I thought through all the categories I wanted my recipes stored under so that I could easily find what I was looking for. Then I took out all my recipes and sorted them into piles all over my family room floor. Of course, I used sticky notes to help me keep my recipe piles straight. As I sifted through recipes, I tossed out those we didn't care for—or ones I no longer wanted to try. If we had favorite recipes in cookbooks, I made a copy of the recipe and added it to my binder piles.

After I had all the recipes sorted and categorized, I put them into three different binders.

> My main dish binder contains my recipes for beef, pork, poultry, seafood, pasta, rice, pizza, soups and stews, crockpot, and casserole dishes

> My side dish binder contains recipes for beverages, appetizers and snacks, breakfast and brunch, breads and muffins, sides and veggies, salads, preserves, sauces and gravy, and miscellaneous recipes

> My dessert binder contains recipes for cookies, brownies and bars, cakes, pies, fruit desserts, frozen desserts, and other desserts

I used tabbed dividers with pockets in them so I could easily stash any stray recipes that I found. I placed large recipes in plastic sheet protectors and used three-hole-punched plastic photo organizers to hold all my smaller recipe cards.

You can tweak this system however you'd like. The categories I created for my binders reflect the types of recipes I have, so your categories may be different from mine. However, what I love about it is that I'm no longer losing recipes, and I can quickly find what I'm looking for when planning meals for the week.

My "Easy Meal" Binder System

Before I had my third child, I put together a list of all the easiest meals I could think of for breakfast, lunch, and dinner as a resource for my mom, who was coming to help out. Don't laugh, but I even wrote down meals like a jar of marinara sauce with pasta, tacos, boxed macaroni and cheese, canned chili with boxed cornbread, grilled cheese with canned tomato soup, and rotisserie chicken with rice.

Through the years, I've added more easy dinner ideas and simple recipes to the list (including all our favorite crockpot recipes). Eventually, this easy meal list of recipes made its way into its own binder (the recipes in this binder are photocopies of recipes from my three large binders). When I feel too tired to think of what to plan for our weekly meals, I often pull out this binder. My easy meal binder has saved the evening more times than I can count.

My Meal Planner System

Over ten years ago, I received a little pad of meal planners as a gift. What I liked about it was that each sheet had space to create a meal plan on one side and space for a shopping list on the other side. However, it was small and only had room to plan meals for five days. Eventually, I decided to create my own meal planning printout. When it's time to go to the store, I sit down with my easy meal binder (if I know we are going to have a crazy week) or my main dishes binder and pick out dinner recipes for the next week. If I'm planning for a special event or to make dessert one night, then I might reference one of the other binders too. I may also include a new meal or two to try from whatever cookbook I'm going through at the time. As I write out the meals for the week, I make my grocery list at the same time.

My Six-Week Meal Rotation System

This system is good for those who don't like the idea of re-inventing the meal planning wheel every week, and it's just like it sounds. To use this system, simply create six weeks of meal

TOOLBOX TIP

Most weeks you'll see "B4D" listed on our meal plan. This stands for "breakfast for dinner." It's one of our favorite meals of the week. We make a combination of something with protein (like eggs, sausage, or ham) and something tasty (like pancakes, waffles, or muffins). It's easy and it's fun!

TOOLBOX TIP

Speaking of planning for meals, here's an efficiency tip for hosting: the night before a party or holiday dinner, I get out all the serving dishes and trays that will be used—and label them with sticky notes. Yes! Sticky notes to the rescue again. I learned this handy-dandy trick from my mom-in-law. This helps me not only to make sure everything I plan on serving has a dish and gets put out but also allows for friends and family to help and know exactly what goes where.

plans. I used to have a four-week rotation list, but I found that some of the meals became too boring and switched to a six-week rotation. I use this system from time to time when I know I'll have a busy season coming and just want things preplanned.

My Freezer Meal System

I'm a big fan of freezer meals. I can't always talk myself into a big, monthly "fill my freezer" day to make a ton of freezer meals at once; I only do that when I'm expecting a crazy season. However, I have found that it's easy to double a recipe and then prepare half of it for dinner that night and put the ingredients for the second meal into a freezer bag to store. It takes no more effort to brown two pounds of ground beef than it does one pound, for example. This saves me the meal prep I'd need to do if I were to make the meal from scratch another night. After a few weeks of doing this, I have myself a nice little stockpile of freezer meals to defrost and toss in the crockpot or oven.

YOU'VE GOT THIS!

Regardless of how your house is designed, basic organization and "station" prep can help you increase your efficiency in your kitchen. You've probably heard it said that "The way to a man's heart is through his stomach." Well, there's some truth to that. Good food makes us all happy. So why not create a plan for feeding everyone in your family with some good food? Meal prep and cooking don't have to be complicated. Just plan for simplicity.

Unlocking Joy

1. **What area in your kitchen needs a better system?** Which organization system can you try out this week to make your kitchen more efficient?

   _____

   _____

   _____

2. **Which meal planning system looks like the easiest one for you to try out first?**

   _____

   _____

   _____

Laundry Systems

Unburying Yourself from the Piles

There is no shortage of advice on the "best" way to do laundry. However, as I pointed out earlier, most advice conflicts. One expert homemaker will say to do all your laundry in one day. But what about larger families that can't possibly get all their laundry done in just one day? Another expert will recommend doing one load per day, every day. But the thought of a never-ending onslaught of laundry makes some people quake in their boots.

Depending on your family size and the season of life you are in, one of these options might be perfect for your family. Yet, as we've been discussing, every family is so different. Right now, all but one of my kids does their own laundry—and I am paying Wade (age eleven) to help Caitlyn (age six) with her laundry. I pay him two dollars if he can get his sister's load completely done: washed, dried, folded, and—wait for it—put away in twenty-four hours. It amazes me that I often find everything done except for that last step. So close, but not quite done. In my lifetime, I've never seen laundry put itself away. It does magically become unfolded and tossed around a room if not put away, but never the opposite.

Now, please don't fret if your kids are too young to train to do their own laundry. Through the years I've discovered some ways to streamline this task, and I am going to share them with you. I'm warning you, though: I break rules. But if you are like me, when you see how well this works you won't care that Emilie Barnes or some other homemaking expert told you that there was a "right" way to do things.

Techniques to Simplify Your Laundry Days

Ditch your perfectionism.

I guarantee that most people are not going to come and inspect your linen closet to make sure your sheets are folded perfectly. Done and out of sight is the goal.

Teach your kids to do their own laundry.

And when you do, remember the first point in this section. They are not going to do things perfectly at first. However, with some practice, even your little kids will become good at folding and putting clothes and towels away. For kids, folding things in half and "matching" corners is fun. I first teach my littles how to fold rags and hand towels, then move on to folding underwear and socks. My toddlers also liked helping me move laundry from the washer to the dryer and getting to push the button to start the load.

Do laundry every week.

Don't "save" laundry for more than a week, because when you skip a week you'll end up with a TON of laundry to fold and put away when you finally get to it. Big loads mean more work. In my case, it means I have to dig deep to motivate myself to get it all done. It is possible to get one or two loads completely done and put away in one day if you keep your loads small and manageable.

Assign everyone a day to get their laundry done.

If you have little kids who can't do their own laundry yet, their laundry will still have an assigned day to be done by you or an older sibling (again, this is a paid chore in our house). Be sure to add everyone's sheets and towels to the calendar too.

Laundry should be done no more than once a week by each person.

I have a few kids who seem to be doing laundry every few days. When that happens, it starts to throw everybody off since we have assigned days. Sometimes this gives me a clue that my kids are outgrowing their clothes—or just picking favorites to re-wear.

Have your kids wash everything on cold.

I told you I am a rule breaker! This allows my kids to do all their laundry in one load. My older boys sometimes divide their clothes into two loads if they have enough whites to wash. But for the most part, all my kids' clothes get washed on cold. I will admit that my husband and I sort our clothes into three loads. We just sort them a bit differently . . . more rule breaking . . .

Sort clothes by water temperature and "bleed factor."

Forget about the typical "whites, brights, and darks." If your "brights" are going to bleed, then they belong in the "cold" basket. I suggest: cold, warm, and hot. Darks and brights go into the cold basket. Light-colored clothes that won't bleed can be washed on warm. Whites will get washed on hot, possibly with bleach if you have all plain white clothes in the mix.

Change your buying habits.

You may want to consider not buying so many white clothes for kids. White clothes look dingy over time when washed with colored clothes, even on cold. To offset this you could wash your kids' white items with yours. Also, consider buying clothes made from materials that are easier to wash and don't require special handling.

Throw delicates in lingerie sacks.

If you have clothes that require special handling or shouldn't go in the dryer, put them in zippered, mesh lingerie bags. Teach everyone in the house to make sure to never put clothes in those sacks in the dryer. When someone is doing their load right behind you, you don't have to worry about your line-dry clothes being tossed in the dryer. Do be sure to remind them to take these clothes out and lay them flat versus leaving them in the sacks to mildew.

Keep your lingerie sacks with your hamper.

To save myself a step on laundry days, I toss clothes that require a lingerie sack directly into the sack before I put them into my hamper. I have three large sacks that I keep hanging next to my three hampers in our bathroom: one for whites, one for lights, and another for brights and darks. When I grab a hamper to wash, I just zip the sack and throw it on top of my pile to take to the washer. I also keep a basket full of different-sized mesh sacks on top of my washing machine for the rest of the family to use.

Do you have similar sized, same-gender kids? Don't wash their clothes together!

I wasted so much time looking at labels to see whose clothes were whose when my boys were little. It made folding and putting away their clothes take forever. Finally, I figured out that keeping their clothes as separated as possible and washing them in different loads cut back my laundry time significantly.

Identify where you usually fail in the laundry cycle.

Getting it into the washer? Switching it to the dryer? Pulling it out of the dryer? Folding it? Putting it away? It's totally okay if you answered, "Yes! All of it!" It just makes me love you that much more. You are honest and, sweet friend, the struggle is real. Figuring out where in the process you drop the ball makes it easier to figure out ways to tweak what you are doing. You may need to start your loads earlier in the day or use a timer to remind yourself to switch the loads, but there are solutions.

Use timers.

I don't always hear the buzzer on my washer or dryer with all the commotion in my home. Sometimes I set the timer on my oven or on my phone to remind myself to switch loads or to pull a load out of the dryer while it is still hot. One tip is to use a timer that doesn't ring once and turn off. You want it to truly remind you to switch the clothes.

Fold laundry as you take it out of the dryer, even if you are in a hurry!

This was a game changer in helping me to get my laundry done in one day. I just make myself fold it right out of the dryer—even when I'm busy. Fold the big things first, like towels. You will feel like a success because it will seem like you're going fast.

Your brain will thank you. Remind yourself that there is less need for an iron if you fold things immediately. Of course, it's important to make sure you have a place to fold clothes in the laundry room.

Bring hangers to the laundry room with your laundry.

Hang up clothes straight from the dryer. Consider investing in a small over-the-door laundry rod to put your hangers on. This will save you time, since there is no need to fold clothes that will be hung up later.

I used to stack all the hang-up clothes flat and take them upstairs. However, I found that I would leave them in that stack until I'd wear them. So getting them on hangers immediately really helps me to stay focused and to finish fast.

Stack clothes in "put away" piles.

Don't mix your stacks! You are just creating more work for yourself when you stack all your clothes in one pile. It means you'll have to take time to separate or sort things again when you put them away. Stack according to final location. If jeans and shorts are put in different places, then stack them separately. This is especially important if you are doing more than one person's laundry at the same time. I create different piles for my husband's clothes and my clothes when I'm doing our laundry.

Pull like items out of the dryer in order.

First, I pull out all the towels and stack them in the bottom of my laundry basket. Then, I pull out everything that needs to go on a hanger and hang them on the rod behind the laundry room door. Next, I fold all the jeans, then boxers, then T-shirts, and lastly the socks and my underwear. That feels like TMI with the underwear talk, but we all wear it, right?

Have "all hands on deck" if your family has been on vacation or away for a time.

This is the one time when I do our entire family's laundry together, sorted by water type. As each load is done, I break my own "fold as it comes out of the dryer" rule and dump the clothes in the middle of the family room floor. Then we all start by separating everyone's clothes into individual piles. Next we have a little folding party and race to get the laundry folded before the next load is done.

This is not something I suggest doing on a regular basis; however, sometimes it is the most efficient way to get multiple loads done and ready for the next week. Don't forget to set your timer so you can stay on top of each load—and get as much done as possible. I have also used this technique when we have had colds or flus and I am trying to disinfect the house.

If you are potty training, buy more underwear and rubber sheets.

Yes, you'll be doing extra laundry during this season. However, I've found that it helps to have plenty of underwear on hand when we have a new "big kid" coming up the ranks. I also cover the bed sheets (and couches in the early stages) with soft rubber sheets that I get at a fabric store. This saves me from having to strip the entire bed down to the mattress in the middle of the night when there are accidents. I can just change the rubber sheet. I also train my kids to put "pee-pee" pants in the laundry room sink (to avoid finding them hiding in random places in the house).

YOU'VE GOT THIS!

Laundry is one of those crazy tasks that we can't seem to get around. We get it all done and put away, and we feel great—but when we turn around, it's back! It's like a *Groundhog Day* repeat. As much as I don't enjoy doing laundry (who does?), I've learned how to do it efficiently. I encourage you to find ways to tweak the tips here and to try out other laundry systems in order to see what works best for you and your family. If you're feeling like you are constantly buried in laundry, then it may just be time to look for different ways to do it.

Unlocking Joy

1. **How have you been doing laundry?**

_____

_____

_____

2. **Go through and circle the tips and systems that you want to try for your family.** Which one will you try first?

_____

_____

_____

3. **How will you divide up your laundry days?**

_____

_____

_____

* Be sure to check out my website for more fun laundry tips and tricks! Just type "laundry" into the search bar at **KristiClover.com**.

Phase III

THE **FINISHING TOUCHES**

Bringing It All Together
to Create a Home You Love!

CHAPTER

18

Making Your Home Both Functional and Fabulous

Breathing Life and Beauty into Your Home

Throughout this book we've been focusing on how to build efficiency and intentionality into our homes. We've laid the foundation with fundamental rules that give us more order for our home life. We've put up a framework to support the structure of our home with systems that will bring about lasting change. Now in this final chapter, we're going to discuss how to bring life to our homes by personalizing our spaces and adding a little dose of pretty. I call this the art of making our homes "functional and fabulous."

> You don't have to sacrifice beauty in your home as you are getting organized. In fact, the less chaotic your house is, the more the beauty of your home can stand out.

It's easy to think we can't be happy in our homes unless the stars of a design program show up on our doorstep and remodel our houses with all the latest and greatest gadgets. While that would be incredible and fun, it is possible to breathe new life into the walls of your home without that kind of help. (I will say that if a design team from HGTV does show up, don't turn them away. Welcome them in and bake them some cookies as they toil away in your home—then send them to my house.) Again, you don't have to go to extremes to enjoy your home and to add a touch of "wow." **We're going for lived-in and lovely!**

Investing time to purposefully decorate your home by adding some finishing touches is helpful in maintaining tidiness. I find that areas I've taken the time to make look beautiful I also keep clean. Don't ask for scientific evidence for this. I've just noticed that I get so much enjoyment out of a pretty room that I am motivated to keep it looking good. Don't neglect this important step, and be sure to add some intentional beauty to your home.

Make Your Vision a Reality

Earlier I talked about praying for a vision for how to best use and organize my home. Well, I also pray for inspiration as to how to create a beautiful environment where people will want to come and gather. I pray for diligence to stay on top of the big and little tasks that creating a life-giving home requires. I also pray for a vision for each room of my home. How can I best stage a room to not only make it functional but also add an element of charm to it? What can I change out to give a room a brand-new feel and a little extra pop of color and texture?

You may already be familiar with vision boards. These are typically large bulletin boards or poster boards used to collect pictures and ideas for a project or goal. Interior decorators use vision boards frequently. They grab samples of fabric, carpet, and paint colors to create a picture of how everything will work together. You can do the same thing, just a bit simpler, by creating digital "vision boards" using Pinterest boards, Instagram bookmarks, or a file on a digital notebook app. For example, when I see home decor I love, I either snap a picture with my phone or take a screenshot of the image, then drop it into my home-decorating ideas folder in my notebook app.

A lot of the interior decorating I've done within my home has come from ideas I collected while walking through model homes and home stores or flipping through home decor magazines. Inspiration is everywhere. Just add your own flair and personal touch to what you see around you or online. You can even go "old school" and create an actual vision board. Get swatches of fabric, magazine clippings, and print pictures—and have fun with it. It's up to you. Just get a feel for what you like and dislike and start looking for ways to implement decorating and design elements into your space.

Personalize Your Space

Your home should reflect the unique interests and personalities of those residing within it. Be sure to personalize each room of your house. If your family enjoys hiking, traveling, or playing at the beach, find ways to have those activities represented in your decor. Maybe you do this by hanging family photos from your adventures or setting out shells, rocks, or pinecones that you collected on your journey. Put your collections in mason jars with a nice label of where you found them. Frame your plane ticket along with your favorite photo from a trip you took. Be sure you don't allow your treasures to become clutter, though. Find ways to display them instead of having them haphazardly lying around taking up shelf space.

Get creative with how you allow your home to be *characterized* by the *characters* who live under its roof. Don't be afraid to display silly moments caught on film or strange memorabilia that will spark a fun memory. If your child loves art, then make sure their artwork and clay creations adorn your bookshelves and walls. Put up shelving or get shadow boxes to show off your collectibles and family heirlooms. These are all creative ways to add a "fingerprint" of everyone in the house—possibly right next to actual sticky fingerprints.

Another way to personalize your space is by showcasing your favorite quotes, poems, or verses. Look online to find adhesive vinyl lettering of quotes you like that you could display on a wall, or look for artwork of sayings you like. Since faith is a top priority in our family, I "scripturize" my home. Yes, I made up that word, but it works perfectly to describe what I do. I personalize our walls and counters by having beautiful hand-printed Scripture throughout our home. You might even consider putting chalkboard paint on a wall or on the back of a door so that you can switch out an inspirational phrase—or just have a spot for some doodling by some little hands.

Out with the Old, In with the Newly Updated

If you have furniture that is old, outdated, or just not enjoyable anymore, then either get rid of it or change it up. I was recently rearranging a room when I realized the large, overstuffed chair I was trying to make fit had two broken legs and no longer matched the decor! This chair was special. It was my gram's, and I have memories of her sitting in it reading stories to Grant and Blake when they were little before she passed away. However, it had become clutter. Big clutter. (This is where my frugality starts to turn into hoarding.)

We don't typically consider furniture clutter. However, often that's what it can become. If you don't love some of the furniture in your house, whether it's clutter or not, think about replacing it with something new that you will enjoy more—and that might even have extra storage in it. If your budget doesn't allow for a new piece of furniture, then consider updating with throw pillows or even a slipcover to add a splash of color.

Celebrate the Seasons

Traditions are a big deal in our family, and our holiday decor reflects this. My holiday bins are filled with seasonal decorations, books, hand towels, and festive pillows. Some holidays get just a few special candles and knickknacks, but others I go all-out for.

Seasonal decorating doesn't have to be complicated. A bouquet of flowers on your coffee table in the spring; American flags or shells from the beach to adorn a side table in your family room for the summer; beautiful autumn leaves and some small, colorful pumpkins for your fireplace mantel in the fall; evergreen sprigs for the kitchen table during the winter.

My kids absolutely love it when they see me pull out our holiday bins. They know it's time for our traditions to begin . . . and let's not forget the yummy holiday meals and desserts they know are coming.

Decorate with Books

Books are a simple and often overlooked way to decorate your home. Obviously you can keep books on bookshelves, but consider

· · · · · · · · TOOLBOX TIP · · · · · · · ·

I've been accumulating holiday decor for years. Pretty much everything I have was purchased at after-holiday sales. You can get a lot more bang for your buck if you just wait for that day-after sale. In fact, we've purchased most of our big-ticket items (dishwashers, tables, couches) during holiday sales. So keep an eye out for great deals.

> ## · · · · · · · · · TOOLBOX TIP · · · · · · · · ·
> Take photos of each area that you decorate for holidays. It makes it easier to remember how you used all your cute decorations from one year to the next. I usually try to take a picture of the area before I start decorating too, so I remember how I had the house staged before I added all the decorations.

stacking a few of your favorites on side tables. I stand books up on my counters next to birthday decorations when we have books that fit with the theme of the party. I often display a cookbook on my kitchen counter, sometimes keeping it open to a delicious-looking recipe. During the holidays, I set out various-sized books on my mantels and around the house. I store these special holiday books in our holiday bins, so they only come out once a year.

Engage the Senses

When I decorate I try to engage as many senses as possible. What I've learned through the years is that kids learn—*and remember*—things best when you involve as many of their five senses as you can. I want my kids to have wonderful memories of their time at home. I want scents and sounds to trigger happy thoughts of time we've spent with each other.

Sight. Keep in mind that adding too many visual elements or allowing clutter to collect can distract from the visual appeal you are trying to create. However, you can add beauty to your rooms with ease by adding pops of color through paint and throw pillows; incorporating various patterns with fabric on furniture, pillows, and window coverings; or using decorative tile on backsplashes or floors.

You can create dimension to your walls by hanging more than just framed items. Consider mounting three-dimensional pieces like old signs, baskets, metal bins, and interesting jars or vases. Fill those pieces with flowers, greenery, and other appealing items. Using different textured materials—a combination of wood, metal, wicker, woven, or stone decor—also adds visual interest to a room. Consider using knobs and handles with different finishes as well.

Adding dimmer switches and some beautiful light fixtures to your rooms increases the aesthetic appeal as well. Or put a strand of lights on a mantel or some other area of the house where you want to draw attention—and add a little twinkle!

Touch. Cozy couches, plush chairs, and warm, comfy beds are an integral part of creating a pleasant tactile environment where people want to stay awhile. Add texture wherever you can throughout your home. Think about the type of flooring you have, the feel of rugs and pillows—and remember to keep a few soft, fluffy blankets near chairs and couches.

Also, don't forget to fill your home with lots of hugs and kisses too. Steve and I often rub our kids' backs at night when we do bedtime cuddles. And here's an unexpected bonus: our kids are learning to give really good back massages now too!

Sound. Take a moment and listen to the sounds of your home. Do you have a lot of unwanted buzz and noise clutter? I try to shut off as much negative noise as I can, and one way I do that is to make sure everyone is tech-free when we're sitting around the table and when we're hanging out together in the evenings.

I try to add intentional sounds to my home that create the kinds of memories I want my kids to have. Laughter is probably my favorite sound to have filling my home. Steve and I try to plan as much fun into our days as possible—even if we have to tickle the laughter out of our kids. And since we're a fairly musical family, our home often has the sound of someone singing, playing the piano or guitar, or streaming music through a portable speaker.

Taste. Food is a great way to add fun to just about anything you do. We aren't going for a Willy Wonka factory with chocolate streams, or edible walls like the old woman's house in *Hansel and Gretel*, so please don't hang food on your walls for your children to nibble on. Do, however, be intentional about the food you have in your home. Keep your pantry stocked with staples for meals and snacks. Be sure to include everyone's favorite meals in your meal plan from time to time too. A picnic at the park or in the backyard, kettle corn for a movie night, peppermint tea on a rainy day, chili for Super Bowl parties, and traditional meals for holidays are all ways to create memories and a special experience within the nonedible walls of your home. A bowl of lemons or apples on the counter adds color, scent, and potential for taste to your home decor too.

Smell. The sweet smell of baked goods or a delicious meal roasting in the oven are great for engaging your family's olfactory senses. However, there are lots of other ways to create good smells around your house. We love diffusing essential oils in our home. I also enjoy using scented candles, soaps, lotions, and bath salts. And don't overlook the odor of your cleaning products. They contribute to the smell throughout your home too. Make sure you use products that have scents you and your family like and that don't clash with each other. And, yes, make sure you have an air freshener of some sort in each bathroom in the house.

Bring the Outside Elements In

There is just something special when you bring the allure of outdoor elements like earth, air, fire, and water into your indoor space. It's an easy way to incorporate additional touches of beauty and texture into you home.

Potted plants and fresh-cut flowers add a hint of *earthy* freshness to your home. Don't be afraid to extend your horticultural decorations to more than just your counter space. Use pretty vases or attractive baskets to display flowers or greenery on shelves, walls, and throughout your home.

Candles bring in the element of *fire* and help to create a warm and welcoming environment. Even a simple dinner made of pizza and carrot sticks can feel fancy when there are candles on the table. When you build a fire in the fireplace on a cold night, hopefully accompanied by a mug of hot chocolate and marshmallows, it instantly adds a cozy glow to the room.

Living in California has taught me to love and appreciate the beauty of *water* and the ocean. While we don't have an ocean view from our San Diego home, we do have a pool that has a waterfall feature. I love to open the windows and let the breeze in to get *air* flowing through the house—and to listen to the sound of the fountain as its water hits the rocks. But you don't have to have a pool or oceanfront property to add water into your decor. For example, aquariums are beautiful and kids love them. From time to time we get fish and enjoy watching them swim around. We've even kept a frog aquarium on our counter so that we could watch the entire metamorphic process take place from eggs to tadpoles to little frogs . . . that blended in too well with our countertops when they escaped.

THE FINAL WALK-THROUGH

You did it! You made it all the way through to the end. You are officially a M.O.M.!
A **Master Organizer of Mayhem!**

While you've come to the end of this book, your organizational story doesn't end here. It's ongoing, so use this book as a reference whenever you feel stuck or like life is getting chaotic again. Sometimes we just need little reminders of the steps to take to get on top of the craziness that managing a house can bring. You may need to review a chapter or two here and there—and start tweaking again.

I'm so excited for you and your family—and for your home! Just as parenting is a never-ending job, so is managing your mayhem and staying organized. My hope is that as you apply the rules, tips, and systems covered in this book, you'll discover that your days and weeks are running more efficiently—and that you will embrace your inner organizer and not let her run and hide again.

I wrote this book in order to encourage and inspire you in the management of your home. I want your home to be a place where you and your family want to be—and where your friends will want to visit and hang out for a while.

Don't believe the lies that you have to be perfect and have it all together, or that your house has to be perfect and put together all the time. Grace, my sweet friend! Give yourself grace. Remember, most moms struggle with keeping their house organized. It's hard work! Focus on the little steps you can take every day to make lasting changes in your home. **You will conquer the chaos and be the best M.O.M. that you can be!**

Blessings and joy,

Kristi Clover

P.S. I hope you have already started exploring all the resources for you and your home that I have on my website:

> Most of my home-related material can be found linked at **KristiClover.com/Home**. I have videos and blog posts filled with tips and how-tos.
> Hopefully, you've also taken advantage of all the easy-to-use printables I designed to go along with the chapters in this book. You can access those at **KristiClover.com /MOMPrintables**.

> Also, don't miss out on a fun **"M.O.M.s Night In"** with your friends! This really is a great way to not only start implementing the tips and techniques in this book but also to add an element of fellowship (and accountability). If you head over to **KristiClover.com/MOMsNightIn** I'll send you a little video introduction for your event and all the details for planning it.

Take Note!

As you read through this book, I encourage you to jot down notes and ideas about tips and techniques you want to try in your own home. If there are any details that you want to be sure to remember, use this space to keep your thoughts in one place.

_____

_____

_____

_____

_____

_____

_____

_____

_____

_____

_____

Take Note!

Take Note!

Take Note!

Take Note!

Acknowledgments

Steve, my awesome husband: I can't believe I get to be your wife. Thank you for always believing in me and supporting me in all my crazy, creative endeavors. Thanks for holding down the fort on evenings and weekends when I had to get writing done. Our kids have no idea just how lucky they are to have you for a dad. I, on the other hand, know exactly what a blessing you are to have as my husband. I love you! (Remember, it's okay to be afraid of how much you love me.)

Grant, Blake, Wade, Ashlyn, and Caitlyn, my incredible kids: you are all truly the best! Thanks for your patience and support as I worked so hard to write this book. Thank you for celebrating every victory along the way with me. This book is what it is because of you . . . both in all the practice I've gotten through the years of figuring out how to best manage our "mayhem" and because of your love and encouragement. Grant and Blake, an extra-big thanks to you for the extra babysitting you did during the writing of this book. Wade, thanks for playing with the girls and keeping them entertained. Ashlyn and Caitlyn, thanks for keeping me well supplied with cuddles. I love you all more than hula pie and to infinity and beyond and back.

Mom: thank you for your enduring encouragement. You have always been my greatest cheerleader. Your love and support mean the world to me. I love you beyond words and am so grateful to have such a wonderful (and incredibly talented) mom! Not to mention the fact that it's been your influence that has sparked my passion for writing and all things fun and creative. Thank you for providing my first glimpse of what it looked like to make a home a welcoming place for others to gather.

Mom and Holly, my Clover family: you have no idea the impact that you have both had on my life. (Dad too! Man, I miss him.) You were the ones I have watched through the years and taken mental notes on how you managed your homes and your families. I had no clue what married life looked like or how to parent multiple kids. It's been such a blessing to be part of your family.

Carol, my prayer warrior godmother: thank you for all your prayers, encouragement, and support through the years. What a blessing to have you as a role model in my life. Your love for others, commitment to pray, and ability to point me back to the Word have been so instrumental in my walk with the Lord. I know that this book is a reality because of your prayers.

Janet Grant, my agent: thank you for all the work you did to make this book come to fruition. Your wisdom and advice through this whole process has been so appreciated. You made every step of the way, from our first discussion about this project to getting this book published, so much better than I ever could have dreamed.

Liz Heaney, my editor: I had no idea what an incredible impact an editor could have on a book. Thank you for your *amazing* advice and for pushing me to make this book the best it could be. Your little encouraging notes and comments throughout the manuscript made the editing process more enjoyable. Thanks for all the hard work you poured into decluttering my wordiness. It was such an honor to work with you.

Rebekah Guzman, my editor: thank you for getting excited with me about this book and for all that you've done to bring this book to print. A big thank you to the whole Baker Publishing Group team too. Everyone in the marketing and sales departments, thanks for making every last detail of this book come together so beautifully.

Tricia Goyer: you are truly more than a dear friend; you are a mentor and an inspiration. It's because of you that this book is in anyone's hand. You believed in me and gave me the best advice anyone could give an aspiring author: "Just write it!" Thank you for everything!

To all my sweet friends: Renee, Andrea, Danielle, Wendi, Heidi, Sarah, and Shelly, what a gift you all are to me! I can't thank you enough for your encouragement and prayers. Heather and Tara, thank you for asking me to step out in faith and speak at those first MOPS meetings. Michelle, thanks for always coming to watch and support me in the early years of speaking on this topic (and smiling at me from the back of the room).

Christen, my manager and assistant: you are my secret sauce! Thanks for all that you do to hold down my "online fort" (especially while I dropped off the grid to write) and for allowing me to bounce a billion ideas off of you. I couldn't pull off half of what I do without you.

Amy, Donna, and Lisa: thanks for always being there to encourage me and offer me such sound advice through the years. You guys are the best top-secret mastermind friends a girl could have.

To my Simply Joyful community and all my wonderful online friends: thank you for listening, reading, and watching! You never know if anyone will relate to what you have gone through and possibly find encouragement from what you've learned. Thanks for your support . . . and for so patiently waiting for my return from my writing abyss. All the notes I received during that time were treasured.

Most importantly, to my precious Lord and Savior: thank you for your grace and for giving me the words, a deep love for encouraging others, and opportunities to use my passions. You deserve all the glory for anything deemed good and praiseworthy in my life.

. . . and thank *you*, dear reader! I am so thankful for you too. I can't wait to connect more!

About the Author

Kristi Clover is a home organization and efficiency expert. She's also an author, a speaker, and the host of the *Simply Joyful Podcast*. Her passion is to encourage families to find simple ways to bring more joy into their home and life. She loves to share about her adventures in motherhood and home life through a variety of media at **KristiClover.com**. As a mom of five, she's never short on opportunities to "practice what she preaches" in the realm of home organization and #momlife. Kristi lives in San Diego with her husband, Steve, and their five children: Grant, Blake, Wade, Ashlyn, and Caitlyn.

Be sure to connect with Kristi online for an extra dose of encouragement. She's **@KristiClover** on most social media networks.

CONNECT *with*
KRISTI

To learn more about Kristi and get access to free resources to help you master the mayhem of #MomLife, sign up for Kristi's enewsletter and connect with her online!

WWW.KRISTICLOVER.COM

SIMPLYJOYFULPODCAST.COM

 @kristiclover

THE

Simply Joyful

PODCAST
with Kristi Clover

Looking for encouragement and inspiration to bring more joy into your day? Subscribe to the *Simply Joyful Podcast*!

If you could use a little encouragement in your faith, family, home, homeschooling, or just the challenges of day-to-day life—this is the podcast for you! Kristi and her guests discuss practical tips for how to find harmony in relationships, create order in your home, and add a little good ol' fun to your week.

LIKE THIS BOOK?

Consider sharing it with others!

- Share or mention the book on your social media platforms. Use the hashtag **#MasterOrganizerofMayhem**.

- Write a book review on your blog or on a retailer site.

- Pick up a copy for friends, family, or anyone who you think would enjoy and be challenged by its message!

- Share this message on Twitter, Facebook, or Instagram: **I loved #MasterOrganizerofMayhem by @KristiClover // @ReadBakerBooks**

- Recommend this book for your church, workplace, book club, or class.

- Follow Baker Books on social media and tell us what you like.

 ReadBakerBooks

 ReadBakerBooks

 ReadBakerBooks